The Homosexual Question

The Homosexual Question

MARC ORAISON

Translated from the French by
Jane Zeni Flinn

HARPER & ROW, PUBLISHERS
New York   Hagerstown
San Francisco   London

This book was originally published in France by Éditions du Seuil, 27 rue Jacob, Paris, with the title *La question homosexuelle.* © Éditions du Seuil, 1975.

FIRST EDITION

Designed by C. Linda Dingler

Library of Congress Cataloging in Publication Data

Oraison, Marc.
  The homosexual question.
  Translation of La question homosexuelle.
  1. Homosexuality. I. Title.
HQ76.25.O713 1977   301.41'57   76-9993
ISBN 0-06-066396-0 pbk.

---

77 78 79 80 81 10 9 8 7 6 5 4 3 2 1

Contents

Prologue   1

1. Observing Reality   10
2. What Is the Question?   33
3. The Other   43
4. Homosexuality and Society   67

   Cultural Differences   67
      Greek Culture   68
      Islam in North Africa   69
      Hebrew Culture   70

   The World of Prison   74
   Our Western Culture   79
   The Myth of Society   94

5. Human Lives and Morals   97

   The Helping Relationship   97
   Homosexual Tendencies and Marriage   106
   Changing a Mentality   111
   The Moral Question   114
   The Homosexual and Faith   124

The Homosexual Question

Prologue

Homosexuality really *is* a question. It challenges us in different ways, according to our own personalities and relationships. The challenge hits us at the deepest, most hidden level of ourselves: how do we handle our own sexuality? And today, with a knowledge of Freud, we have to admit that the issue is neither simple nor straightforward.

The homosexual question brings a variety of responses; some people react strangely, even violently. In fact one of these reactions finally clinched my decision to write this book. The incident itself is not very important. But it struck me as a sign of such ignorance and such unwillingness to think that I felt I had to communicate what I myself had learned.

I'll often write in the first person. After all, this book reflects the development of my personal ideas, and I expect it to be subjective. I certainly do not pretend to "diagnose" the problem in any definitive way. These are simply my thoughts on the homosexual question, after many years of clinical experience, of conversations and even friendships with homosexuals[1]—men and women—and of numerous discussions with psychologists, social

1. We will see further on the inadequacy and oversimplification in the current use of the term *homosexual*.

workers, clergy, and others in what we call the "helping profes-
sions."

But first let's go back to the incident that prompted me to write.

In October, 1973, at the request of the editors, the following
article appeared in the magazine *Telerama*:

Tuesday, Oct. 2. *Screen Notes:* **"Special Friendships"**

*It is a delicate subject, one that people didn't mention a few years
ago. Today everyone talks about homosexuality, even on television.
Yet the word covers a wide range of experience, and the debate is
growing heated and often confused. We concluded that the most useful thing we could do would be to provide some information and calm
analysis. We didn't feel it was our job to make judgments. Instead we
turned to a specialist in the field, a doctor who is also a priest, Fr.
Marc Oraison:*

During the past few years, in literature, in films, and on television,
a subject that was long taboo has been brought to the public—homosexuality. This is real progress, because homosexuality is a fact of
human life; it would be dishonest or hypocritical to ignore it. But
the new openness carries a built-in risk of oversimplification that leads
to caricature, segregation, or defensiveness. An episode in the recent
broadcast of *God's Madness* was a clear example. It showed a group
of American homosexuals whose lifestyle was so exaggerated that the
broad and complex problem was reduced to one of its minor aspects.

For over twenty years, as priest and psychologist, I have been consulted by five or six homosexuals in an average week. They have been
men and women of all classes and all ages. Knowing them has made
me think, and I hope my conclusions may dispel a few prejudices and
falsehoods. First of all, a man who is homosexual is not responsible
for his situation. He has not chosen it. Thus it would be entirely unfair to censure him, as if homosexuality were a moral defect, his own
fault. It creates some problems for him, which may be more or less
dramatic, more or less obvious; but he is not a *being apart*. Homosexual men and women, in their own way, share the human condition
—and we all know, if we are honest with ourselves, that it is not

easy. In my experience a good many live with their "problem" in the
truly Christian sense, participating in the suffering of humanity, which
becomes meaningful through the Cross of Christ. "In my own body,"
says St. Paul, "I make up what is lacking from the sufferings of Christ."
Viewed in this way, the homosexual is much like the woman suffering
with scruples, the man troubled by an inferiority complex, the heterosexual who has "problems"—sometimes distasteful ones—with his
heterosexuality. Everyone, to some degree, has "problems." The problem of homosexuality is just one among many. Thus the "racism"
that we see so often directed against homosexuals is deplorable.

Words are important here. Homosexuality is not an *illness* in the
usual sense of the term. It is not something that strikes you at a particular moment, and disables you temporarily, or for a long time, or
for the rest of your life. The majority of homosexuals feel "ill at ease"
to some extent, but hardly "ill." We must strongly oppose the all-too-
common tendency to consider homosexuality some sort of "mental
illness." Then again, it is always the *others* who are mad. . . .

But now, what word can we use? I believe we can say that homosexuality is the result of an anomaly of affective and psychological
development rooted in earliest childhood. (Except in very rare cases,
no physical or organic cause can be detected.) A small minority of
homosexuals feel it such a basic element in their unconscious that they
make aggressive claims, scorning heterosexuality as "inferior" or confusing the issue with political ideologies. Few but vocal, they tend
to be true neurotics; and they are no help to all the others who would
sooner just be left alone.

In any case, homosexuality does not exist; it is a word. People
exist—human beings who have homosexual tendencies and who live
with them as best they can. They are individuals as diverse as the
rest of humanity. The "homosexual type" is a fiction, a caricature; I
wonder if those who describe it are not really protecting themselves
from some hidden distress of their own. By contrast, homosexual men
and women often seem completely "average," a bit reserved at most.
People wonder why they stay single. (I might add that it would be
foolish and heavy-handed for their friends to push them into marriage as a "cure." That can lead to real disasters.)

How many people know that a man of the stature of Lyautey[2] was homosexual? There was nothing sordid about it. I knew a forty-year-old man who, at twenty, had been Lyautey's last *grand amour*. The relationship went on for several years, and was as noble and high-minded as Lyautey himself. And the younger man was never disturbed by the memory.

Homosexuality is not an isolated phenomenon. I would like to stress something quite obvious, though it may seem hard to accept. The father of a family does not feel the *same* affection for his son as he feels for his daughter—simply because the first kind is "homosexed" while the second is "heterosexed." This is a normal, common point of departure. But for varied and complicated reasons a child's emotional development may be thwarted; the erotic impulse may not lead to the normal, free desire for the "other." Or perhaps some development occurs, but it is distorted and chaotic. There are also many heterosexuals who are not "normal." . . .

We tend to react spontaneously by *judging* homosexuals. I must confess that twenty years ago I did so myself. Then at last I had to face the facts: two homosexuals *can* have a relationship, though transitory, of real love, even of charity. At the same time, certain heterosexual relationships, even among married couples, have little to do with love. . . . It is not that it is difficult to pronounce judgments; it is impossible.

Only in the human species do we find homosexuality as such. It is one aspect of the universal human tragedy—the deep mystery of ambivalence. We want to attain the fullness of love, but we cannot achieve the liberation from ourselves which could make it possible. The ambiguity of desire, in the broadest sense of the term, is that it is "for the other," at once encountering him as "other," and accepting him as our own reflection. Homosexuality is as old as the world, as old as the human drama. We are all brothers in the chiaroscuro of the path of life.

2. Louis Hubert Gonsalve Lyautey (1854–1934), a French marshal, leader of the Moroccan protectorate, and Minister of War in 1916–17. He was a spokesman for colonialism as a civilizing process, and for social reform at home—Tr.

A couple of weeks later, someone kindly mailed me a copy of the explicit, if not provocative, tabloid *Action Française*. This issue contained the following article:

... To Marc Oraison the removal of a taboo is "real progress." The hypocrisy and dishonesty that banned this subject and led to anti-homosexual racism are out of style today. Bravo, Marc! Since homosexuality is no longer a defect, our streets will swarm with made-up, periwigged creatures. See the graceful gestures, the limp wrists, the stiff legs, the shapely rear ends under the tight pants? There they go, mincing along arm in arm. ...

Thus we are told that the homosexual is not a "being apart." He lives with a problem in "the truly Christian sense, participating in the suffering of humanity, which becomes meaningful through the Cross of Christ." Well what do you know! The sexual act of perverts is a share in the suffering of humanity. The error of such "thinking" is that while humanity may suffer, the homosexual doesn't suffer at all. He enjoys himself. ...

Perversion reaches its peak when the author writes that a father "does not feel the same affection for his son as he feels for his daughter." In case you haven't guessed, the father-son affection is homosexual, while the other is heterosexual. But we'd like to know what sex has to do with the love of parents for their children? The way these fanatics write, you would think that sex is everything, everywhere, to everyone. You would think they found their own pleasure, not in the act of sex, but in the writing of trash. With "normal homosexuality" and "abnormal heterosexuality," it won't be long now before we staunchly praise homosexuality and firmly condemn heterosexuality. ...

The one time a commandment is mentioned, the "new morality" turns it inside out. "Judge not" has never suggested that we should be blind to good and evil. This commandment teaches that all men are brothers before God and that only He has the power to judge them.

We know, of course, that a homosexual is not necessarily responsible for his perversion. But the problem isn't whether or not he is responsible. The problem is that a homosexual—by the example he sets, by the disorder he suggests, by the dissipation he represents—is a danger. From the moment homosexuality becomes a danger, as it certainly is today, we must fight this cancer. We must fight the forces that have led people down such paths—true—but we must also fight the scum who parade these disorders around and sing their praises.

With no offense to Marc Oraison, we *will* judge homosexuality. We will judge these books and periodicals which cart debauchery right into the temple of morality: the Church. We will also judge these vice peddlers who sell their wares at the gate of the temple of purity: youth. Our Lord drove the merchants from the Temple; the likes of Marc Oraison must be exterminated.

My first reaction to this diatribe was to wonder what to make of such anger and such unwillingness to think. From what hidden threat or anxiety could the writer be protecting himself? Why does the question of homosexuality concern him *so much?*

He talks about "God" and the "Church." I wonder what to make of this, too. His attitude reminds me of the character in some novel or other who declared: "I am not a Christian! I am a Catholic!" The phrase speaks for itself.

This article probably created little stir except among a few extremists. But it did make me think. It is almost a caricature of a rather common attitude in our society. Homosexuality is a loaded question, provoking extreme reactions. Many people do reject it as a taboo, just as people in other circles ardently defend it.

The first reaction seems to be much more widespread than the second. But both of them keep us from facing the question with open minds and seeing all its implications—anthropological, social, moral, philosophical, and spiritual. I do not claim to exhaust these subjects; I simply want to contribute what I can.

My own reactions to homosexuality have not always been the same. As a medical student and intern between 1932 and 1943

I had only the usual simplistic and superficial ideas. We whispered discreetly that so-and-so must be "one"; we knew that certain people had "different lifestyles"; we made jokes, good and otherwise. And that was all. As a surgeon I had no reason to face the problem clinically, even if at times I had to operate because of certain anorectal or urogenital consequences. We didn't talk about the homosexual question itself—not seriously. We "classified": there were the homosexuals, and there were the "normal people," two groups clear and simple. And I was certainly not far from assuming that the "homosexuals" were there by some sort of choice, because they were guilty of some moral perversity —an idea which now strikes me as absurd. The only major writing on the subject was André Gide's *Corydon!* I had little to do with psychiatrists. Besides, the revolutionary ideas of Freud had reached only a handful of people, who were considered crackpots.

I really started to examine the issues when I studied moral theology at the Institute Catholique de Paris, during my preparation for the priesthood. First I learned the theories—through my courses, and through books like Hesnard's *Manuel de Sexologie* ("highly recommended reading"). In this way, I encountered the whole new world of psychoanalysis.

Next came my clinical initiation. As a newly ordained priest I began hearing confessions in a parish near the Pigalle in Paris. Four years later, in 1952, I based a small theological work[3] on my experience, never suspecting it could cause such a stir. Among other topics, the book dealt with homosexuality. I approached it in a new way, aiming first at a medical and psychoanalytical study, and then at an open-minded consideration of the moral issues.

3. *Vie Chrétienne et Problèmes de la Sexualité*, Ed. Lethielleux (Paris: 1952). Placed on the Index in 1953. Reissued in 1972 by Fayard-Lethielleux.

The response was swift. Since 1953 I have received a growing flood of requests for consultation, many of them related to the homosexual question. Priests and medical doctors sent me penitents and clients whom they couldn't deal with themselves. Readers of the 1952 book came to see me, then sent me their friends and acquaintances.

This explains the unusual range of my experience. Over a period of twenty years, I have met six or seven people with homosexual problems each week. About a quarter have been women, and three-quarters have been men. Their ages run the gamut; I've seen seventeen-year-olds and eighty-year-olds. But the greatest number are between twenty and thirty-five.

My position happened to be almost unique: priest and physician in ever-closer contact with psychoanalysis. Many people came to see me who would not have considered discussing their problem with a clergyman.[4] Others came who would not have gone to a doctor or a psychoanalyst. When I referred them to therapists most of these clients never followed through.

Several times, as I discussed all this with psychoanalyst friends, we concluded that I was seeing people who would not consult anyone else. In such cases there might be one long conversation, or sometimes two or three. Some people came back to see me after gaps of as long as eighteen years.

I hope I have made my purpose and orientation clear. This book will spell out a position which will perhaps shock certain readers. But I will not challenge traditional ideas just for the sake of argument. As the saying goes, "I know what I am talking about."

For twenty years I have listened to the stories of countless

---

4. In the past eight or ten years things have changed a great deal. More and more priests and ministers have adopted a psychoanalytic point of view. Formerly there were two of us. Today, too, people speak of homosexuality openly, with much less embarrassment.

people struggling with problems of homosexuality. I have tried to understand—not just the stories, but also their impact on me. In the psychoanalytic sense it was "countertransference." Obviously I can no longer think of the homosexual question in the old simplistic, superficial way. "Traditional ideas" were deeply rooted, but they could not stand up to experience. I would like to share the results, subjective as they are, of my personal evolution.

1. Observing Reality

We must always beware of the language trap. Some people automatically base their thinking on certain catchwords and assumptions, so that their vision is distorted from the start. An underlying philosophy can cause even more trouble if it is unstated; it can blind the observer and paralyze any investigation of conflicting data.

The word *Life* is a case in point. To a modern biologist it is an ambiguous term. It carries a rather insidious mental image: "Life in itself," as in Platonic or Scholastic thought, must actually exist somewhere. From a scientific point of view, however, "Life" does not exist. Only living beings exist and can be observed. Through them we can study the molecular and organic structures which distinguish the matter called living from that called nonliving. Of course these structures pose questions of a realm quite other than scientific: problems of origin, causation, and meaning. But if we carefully put aside the Platonic ideas and mythic presuppositions, these questions burst out in a whole new form, without any built-in answers. In fact we are left with no answers at all —no clear, rational responses that reassure the mind and give the false impression that we have understood. (Of course we may then substitute the myth of scientism, as if "Science," like "Life," actually existed somewhere.) Yet we must live with uncertainty if we want to avoid statements and ideas that can become colossally inhuman. What do current expressions like "Respect for Life" or "Respect for Science" really mean? So many crimes are committed or condoned in the name of what must truly be called idols!

I think if we want to approach the homosexual question without bias we must strive for this same discipline. Homosexuality *does not exist*. Human beings exist, and some of them, from their first sexual awakening, have been physically attracted toward persons of their own sex. The only way we can study homosexual attraction is through—and with—these individual men and women. But once we strive to eliminate the idea of "homosexuality in itself," to free ourselves of certain prejudices (literally "judging before knowing"), we are struck by the great diversity and complexity of what we see.

The simplistic, Manichaean view that is still so common just cannot account for the facts. There are not two kinds of people, "the homosexuals and the others." Yet both the "traditional moralists" and the defenders of "persecuted sexual minorities" assume this kind of dualism. Whether in the guise of "Gay Liberation" or crusades for public decency,[1] such thinking can keep us from facing the homosexual question as it really is. It can help maintain a fortress of misunderstanding and conflict in the midst of possible attempts to improve human relations. That would be tragic. Reality, when carefully observed, cannot in any way be reduced to this simplistic dichotomy.

Current vocabulary and its inconsistent usage certainly do not help to clarify matters. Wherever you go, you can hear comments like: "He's one of *them*, you know. . . . He looks like one." What "one of *them*" means, you are supposed to understand. If you ask people of different backgrounds and lifestyles to attach

---

1. The article quoted in the Prologue is a good example.

a name to this innuendo, there will be quite a variety: "queer," "fag," "pervert," etc. The origin of these expressions is often obscure and not very enlightening. The point, though, is always pejorative, or at least ironic and mocking. Then again, a man who says that someone else "is one of *them*" also means, consciously or not, that he himself "is not one." This is classification in self-defense. Some would say that this instinctive classifying is purely a cultural matter, related to "bourgeois morality." Personally I am not convinced. Such a claim strikes me as another oversimplification, which reduces the entire problem to sociology.

The terms applied to homosexuality do not all refer to the same thing. To call someone a "pansy" is humiliating. The speaker suggests that his victim is passive and weak, willing to be "used" (sexually, I mean; there are stronger terms). The word *pederast*, though, means just the opposite: an adult who is attracted to pubescent boys, and who is, himself, active and aggressive.

Sometimes feminine terms are applied to men; more often, it seems, than the other way around. (Why is a strong, mature personality so often confused with masculinity? A woman will be described as "mannish" when she is, in fact, totally feminine—but more talented and forthright than most. Perhaps the others are threatened.) We don't know how most of these expressions originated either, but the image is clear. Such feminine terms as *queen, fairy, femme,* or *tata* suggest a specific class of individuals, few in number but highly "visible." They are caricatures of women, with nervous, affected mannerisms. Their style, carried to its logical extreme, is that of the transvestite.

The only term that can really apply to the problem as a whole is *homosexual*. Unfortunately in most people's minds it has negative connotations. Some homosexual people have therefore proposed the term *homophile*. While this may sound a bit less pejorative, it is also less accurate; in a sense it avoids the issue entirely by eliminating any direct reference to sexuality as such. The suffix *phile* suggests the love of the emotions, or the idea of a favorite activity. Thus we speak of bibliophiles, of philatelists, of francophiles. Homosexuality is not so simple. At the same time the term *homophile* does add an important dimension: more often than people think, homosexual attraction is emotional rather than sensual, marked by real tenderness and even devotion.

In short, if we want a more precise and adequate vocabulary we will have to invent it. But I am not about to undertake the task now. I'll settle for the term *homosexual* as defined in this way: a person beyond puberty who feels sexually attracted, exclusively or otherwise, to people of the same sex.

Here, though, I run into difficulties. For if I want to stick close to reality and to avoid the traps of language, of polemics, of assumptions, how can I say anything meaningful about a subject as diverse as homosexuality?

Perhaps the best course is to introduce you to a series of real people. Their stories are drawn from my clinical experience of the past twenty years, with care, of course, to protect the privacy of those involved. I might add that many of my visitors had no formal religious background at all; they chose to consult me for a variety of reasons.

There was a good middle-class office worker of average intelligence. He came to see me on the advice of his confessor. Conservatively dressed, thirtyish, he looked "like anyone"—just a bit timid, perhaps. He was married and the father of two little girls; he loved his family dearly. His sexual relationship with his wife was quite satisfactory as he described it.

Yet two or three times a week, at the station where he caught the train home to the suburbs, he was driven to roam the urinals in search of partners. Furtive contacts, mutual masturbation in semidarkness, sometimes just petting. (He got in trouble once when he ran across a police decoy.) For him the main thing was *not to know* the partner of the moment; at times it was a real obsession with the *anonymous* phallus. Symbol of what deeper distress?

Though he had no particular sexual problems with his wife, their marriage did not always run smoothly; there were moments of anxiety, personality conflicts. Yet there was really nothing serious. I had two meetings with his wife, at her request, and she confirmed my impression. She was aware of what was going on, and accepted the situation with much love for her husband. Her manner did not strike me as "dominant" or "maternal."

All this happened almost fifteen years ago. I saw the man intermittently for two or three years, for spiritual rather than psychotherapeutic counseling. Then he did not come back. Yet I have the feeling that things worked out for them.

A brilliant man of twenty-four wanted more than anything to marry and have children. He was strongly attracted to women. In fact he was in love, but he seemed to protect himself from knowing it. (This defense mechanism is quite common. To a young man who is still "drifting" in the social and professional world, the woman who arouses his love "disrupts" him in some way; she threatens to draw him out of his comfortable ambivalence.) Occasionally this man would get involved with boys of eighteen or twenty. The affairs didn't go very far, but there were emotional and erotic overtones; all this is much like the "special friendships" of adolescents living in a single-sex environment.

He was not, however, content with this situation; he saw it as transitory and wanted out. He found himself professionally through a satisfying job, and in little more than a year he managed to free himself sexually as well. No longer threatened, he moved into a fully adult heterosexuality and married the woman he loved. (She had waited several years for him.) They had two children. In short, without any formal psychotherapy, he freed himself from chronic episodes of adolescent ambivalence, which were perhaps more marked than usual in his case. Later, when he is about fifty, will this ambivalence return? It is not impossible, but I doubt it.

Stories like this are more common than people think. I am convinced that some people remain "blocked" by guilt and anxiety, or simply by the lack of someone to talk to.

Then there was a man of about forty, highly successful in his social and professional life. Everyone liked him; he was good company. His acquaintances were only surprised that he stayed single, but generally they shrugged it off, telling themselves: "He must have his reasons; after all, it's his business." Very few people knew or even suspected his problem. Yet it was often very painful to him.

He had never, since adolescence, felt the slightest attraction to a woman. His tendencies were exclusively homosexual, and sometimes quite obsessive, with erotic fantasies about young men of twenty or twenty-five. Twice in his life, though, it was different—he fell in love with a boy whom he knew well. Surprisingly enough, each time it was with a heterosexual boy who felt an unproblematical friendship for him. Both times he expressed his own feeling, but not as a demand, and the boy accepted it well. His erotic desires tapered off and practically disappeared, leaving only a deep affection. A sexual relationship was unthinkable; it would have seemed incongruous to *him*. He became the friend of the two new households that were established, and both wives were probably aware of his feeling for their husbands. Both times these relationships worked out well.

In each case he felt a temporary calming of his sexual drives.

He became "continent" as the saying goes, in a way that was natural and effortless. Yet after a few months—somehow in spite of himself—he would return to the transient erotic affairs which left him unfulfilled and bitter.

At twenty-two, R. became a prostitute on the Pigalle. He was a good-looking boy, tastefully dressed, and he usually did well. His background was complex: instability, running away from home, the lure of easy money, etc. Yet he managed to find some sort of physical pleasure and emotional satisfaction in this way of life. As he put it, "I swoon in the arms of a man."

When I saw him again, eight years later, he had changed. He had lived a rather wild life on the fringe of delinquency in France, Italy, and Belgium. Then gradually he had found his vocational niche and returned to France. He was holding down a regular job and enjoying it.

There was no more "swooning in the arms of a man." All that was nothing to him now, just a distant memory. In fact he was living with a woman and they seemed to be getting along well.

The next story may sound strange, but I have known several like it. The man was about thirty-five, and deeply disturbed in his emotional and sexual life—his only relationships were with boys. I saw him often, as a client and as a friend. Although I had strongly urged him to consider formal psychotherapy, he never got around to doing anything about it.

He was violently attracted to boys of fifteen or sixteen who were ambivalent themselves. He met them mainly through "educational" activities in the arts—drawing and sculpture. (One time that led to a criminal charge and two years in prison. This did not apparently resolve his problem.)

One day he told me he was madly in love with a certain Daniel, age seventeen, and couldn't live without him. Daniel was also very attached to him. They had quite frequent sexual relations, with petting and mutual masturbation.

Within a year Daniel made a good start in a trade he liked. He met a girl his own age and they fell in love. He told his friend all about her; when the young couple made plans for their future, the men talked them over in bed. The older man encouraged and helped Daniel despite his own hurt. The wedding took place, and this friend was Best Man.

For the next few years they saw each other often, though all homosexual activity stopped completely. The younger man, whom I met a few times, remembered it only as an episode of the past. He and his wife got along well, and their old friend was a welcome guest. Then gradually they drifted apart. As far as I know, the married couple have no special problems, and are raising two (or three?) children normally.

The man I knew well is now almost fifty. He has since met other boys, and told me about them. But little by little he stopped coming to see me, and I don't know what has become of him.

About twenty years ago I received a request for a consultation from one Jean-Michel, age eighteen. A novel had just appeared—a good one, in fact—whose main character was homosexual. I had written a favorable review; Jean-Michel had read the novel and my critique, and had decided to write me. For several years we saw each other four or five times a year. (He lived in a large city in the provinces, and only rarely came to Paris.)

At this point he was doing very well in his first year at the University. He was an only child left fatherless when he was very young. Anxious, obsessive, and highly intelligent, he was attracted strongly and exclusively to boys about his own age. From time to time he would meet them in the squares or in the seamier parts of town; then he experienced intense guilt, quite in keeping with his obsessive personality. A few times during the years he was seeing me he had some troubles with the police, fortunately minor ones.

After two or three years he decided to begin formal psychotherapy. At the same time he was doing brilliant academic work, and in spite of gnawing anxiety, managed to make a good start in his career.

During three years of analysis he worked out his sexual problems. He "discovered" woman by freeing himself from the mother image, which in his case was neurotic. And he discovered the "woman for himself" at the same time as "himself for the woman." (No doubt during this whole process I was playing the role of a "father figure." He explored all this later with his analyst, who was a woman, and my role seems to have been quite positive.)

At twenty-seven or twenty-eight he married a young woman he had known for several years as a fellow student. She was feminine, intelligent, and keenly intuitive.

They had a good sexual relationship, but as it turned out there were fertility problems. Tests showed that he was the one who was sterile. They sought the best medical advice and treatments, but nothing happened. Just as they had resigned themselves to not having children, she became pregnant. His sperm count was then found to be almost normal and two more children were born; they must be six or seven years old now. Was his earlier sterility psychological in origin? I don't think we can dismiss the hypothesis.

Today the homosexual tendencies are gone. The anxious and obsessive symptoms remain, but they have tapered off and cause little trouble. He is highly successful in his career and has achieved a good balance in his family and social life.

The next story is very different. This man was a priest; he first came to see me around 1960, when he was about forty. He was highly respected in his ministry, dedicated, understanding, and inspiring. A few personality problems—he was a bit nervous and touchy—did not hamper his thoroughly successful career.

Nobody knew what was torturing him. When he finally confided in me, it was the first time he had ever managed to discuss it openly. Since his earliest sexual awakening his tendencies had been exclusively homosexual. He had always fought these tendencies, yet shortly after leaving the seminary he had his first affair. There were times ever since when he could not resist the need for homosexual encounters; afterwards he felt overwhelming guilt, which was more emotional than rational.

His partners were young men whom he met in squares or cafés far from home. He never revealed his true identity. There would be a short embrace and mutual masturbation, without much further acquaintance. (This seems to be quite typical of homosexual life.)

He suffered intensely for ten years, but could never fully conquer the problem that was warping his personality. What made him suffer was a sort of contradiction in his life—his ideals and his image in the eyes of others, versus these drives that he could not control. Then he began to feel less guilt-ridden, since it was clear he had not *chosen* to be this way.

Gradually he worked toward a spiritual interpretation of his problem. He often thought of the letter of St. Paul where Paul mentions a "thorn in the flesh" that frees him from pride. When he did meet a partner, he strove for at least a minimal sort of human relationship; that is, he took an interest in the other in a way that was not merely sexual.

For several reasons psychoanalysis was out of the question. So for some years I saw him on an occasional basis, helping him as best I could to work out his own development. He came to a certain inner peace. Life was still painful, of course, but he got himself together enough to cope with his faith and his ministry. At last the irresistible drives seemed to come more rarely.

After several years he stopped coming to see me. I assumed that he no longer needed to, and that he was getting along without help. This must have been true, because he has since asked me to take part in two or three pastoral activities without ever mentioning his problem.

I tend to think of the next three people together. In fact they knew each other to some degree. At the time when I knew them, they were members of a rather informal, sprawling band of street people with whom I had managed to get involved.

Let's call the first one "Toto," since I knew him only by his last name. (This is not the real one.) His pals often added the epithet "the Nut," which is significant coming from boys who were disturbed enough themselves. I knew him well, and he was able to confide in me. He didn't have much home life: his mother was sickly, and his father had vanished.

Toto had three dominant traits. He had an obsession with revolvers, which he stole when he couldn't resist their fascination. He was totally unstable in his character and "career," if we can apply the term to his invariably brief attempts as a bartender or waiter. His tendencies were exclusively homosexual and passive; his chief desire was to be penetrated, so he served as a willing prostitute. He was eighteen or nineteen years old at the time.

For several years I saw him occasionally, or got news of him from those of his friends I was still seeing. One or two spells in prison for theft punctuated a life that was unstable at best. His "work" was still varied and ill-defined. He frequented a bar where some big shots of the underworld seemed to gather.

After two or three years of silence I happened to learn that he was again in jail. This time, though, it was for something serious: attempted murder. He sent me a letter from prison, but

made no mention of what had happened. It was quite by accident that I already knew about it.

He had met a man of thirty or thirty-five, also homosexual, and
they had started going together. After a few months, as often
happens in such situations, this man had left him and found another boy. One evening Toto met up with him again in his car
near the Pigalle. He pulled out a revolver and pointed it at his
lover, "to scare him." Somehow or other the gun went off. The
friend found himself in the hospital; a bullet had passed through
his neck, but had fortunately touched nothing vital. Toto found
himself back in jail. I don't know if he is out yet.

Still more tragic is the story of Michel G. I didn't know him
well personally, as I saw him just two or three times. But I knew
quite a lot about him from his "pals."

He had been abandoned as a child, taken in by a welfare
agency, and raised in a series of foster homes. His foster families
were not the best. He grew up in increasing emotional isolation,
with a sort of despairing hatred of himself. At eighteen he was
turned loose in Paris. There he picked up odd jobs and more or
less joined a gang. Mostly, though, he went back and forth between the Pigalle and Saint-Germain-des-Prés, looking for men
who were willing to have him. For as he told me himself around
this time, he did not turn to prostitution just as a way to earn
money without working. It was really to meet men who "were
willing to have him." Being a gigolo was the only way he was
able to feel wanted. His own sexual inclinations were ambivalent.

Then he was caught up in the web of the drug traffic. He
played a very minor role, but started smoking hashish himself.
He got eighteen months in jail. Upon his release, of course, he
returned to Saint-Germain-des-Prés. He met a "friend" there, and
they left together for a tour of Italy or Spain. After they re-

turned the friend dropped him. Back in his inexorable solitude, he again took to the streets. Soon he was again used by the drug pushers, and he went back to prison. Now his isolation was total and permanent.

I learned the last episode from an article in *Le Monde*: a silent suicide in his jail cell. They found him one morning, hanged by an electric cord he had ripped out. Without a word, without a letter; he had nobody to contact.

I remember that this was about the same time as the suicide of Montherlant.[2] I could hardly endure the flood of foolishness, snobbery, and philosophico-literary drivel that this great man had prompted by such a spectacular exit.

The description of the third boy will come as a surprise, since he was not a homosexual in the usual sense of the word. Of the three, he was the one I knew best; we had many long conversations. He was highly gifted, but at the same time severely imbalanced. He lived in a constant state of fear, uncontrollable panic that led him to strange and aggressive behavior.

His childhood was peculiar. The son of a prostitute and a North African, he was quickly placed in a foster home, and was not taken back by his mother until he was nearly seven. He then went to live with her in a room of a sordid transient hotel in one of the most miserable sections of Paris. There she plied her trade, in front of him when he was not at school. Her clients were exclusively North Africans of unsavory backgrounds.

At about twelve he stole a little money—ten francs—from the hotel cash register to go to the movies. He was caught, and with

2. Henry Marie Joseph Millon de Montherlant (1896–1972). Montherlant was a writer of novels, essays and plays which revealed different facets of his own egocentric personality. His virile aristocratic point of view was opposed to a democratic age he called effeminate. Dreading blindness, he committed suicide on September 21, 1972—Tr.

his mother's agreement sent to a reform school (in the sense of the word twenty years ago). For six years he lived in this place, rigidly disciplined, with other boys as disturbed as he. They trained him as some sort of mechanic, a trade that did not appeal to him. His mother came to see him only two or three times in all.

That was how he got to know Michel G., who spent a few years at the same place, and was about his age. With the help of a few pals he occasionally sodomized Michel. Yet at sixteen he managed to escape from the school and to seduce a local girl of fifteen, getting her pregnant.

At eighteen he, too, was turned loose on the streets of Paris. He tried living with his mother, but could only stand it for a few weeks. Then he turned to a vagabond life, very alone yet mingling with the street people who gathered in one of the local squares. There were thefts, hard knocks, brawls; a few tries at work were soon abandoned.

Returning from military service (which he spent in the Sahara toward the end of the Algerian War), he got married and made some attempts to start a normal life. There were two children in five years. But it was a chaotic existence, marked by some major burglaries and violent brawls. He was not caught, but he was known to the police. Living with his wife became intolerable and they separated. Then he met another girl, seduced her, and sent her out to walk the streets. For more than a year, he did nothing else. Then he went back to "working," always on the fringes of crime. I don't believe he ever got involved with drugs, but he soon became an alcoholic with severe attacks of delirium tremens. The girl, with his approval, had a child and left the street to go to work. But their life together became unbearable. She too left him, under really tragic circumstances.

From a sexual standpoint this boy was truly obsessive, though he was attracted exclusively to women. Quasi-compulsive mastur-

bation, prostitutes, casual girlfriends. He had a taste for deflow-
ering young girls, and this brought him some notorious troubles
with the police.

Yet he absolutely could not *live* with a woman, that is integrate
her into his world as a human being and life partner. Instead he
surrounded himself with "pals." He would make his successive
women put up with them, and then go out with his pals for end-
less rounds of the seamier bars. There was always a favorite,
weaker than himself, whom he didn't let out of his sight; he
would protect and exploit him at the same time. Like him, the
boy tended to be "lost," and cut off from whatever family he
might have. At the time when I often visited his first household,
I noticed a recurrent scene: the young woman would be sitting
on a chair off to one side, while he and his pal sat next to each
other on the sofa, his hand resting on the boy's knee. I am sure,
however, there was no sexual relationship between them.

His suffering was old and complex in its origins. But at this
point it was rooted in a contradiction which was tearing his sexuality apart. Though erotically heterosexual, he was emotionally
homosexual, unable to face the duality of marriage and to find
his place there.

This story seems especially significant for two reasons. First
of all it shows the complexity of the problem and the ambiguity
of the term *homosexual*. Second, it is important to note that this
man had never known any sexual prohibitions, in any case not
before puberty. We could not say that this helped him to find
himself. We will come back to the issue of "prohibitions"; on
this point certain homosexual leaders show a strange ignorance
of psychological fact.

Contrast brings a subject to life. So I will now introduce the
following example.

Pierre was twenty-two. He came to see me on the advice of a

school director, but the decision was clearly his own. He had been a counselor and sometime student at this establishment. Then people learned that "things were going on" in the dormitory, and that for several months he had been having a love affair with a sixteen-year-old boy. (I might note that this sort of thing is not unusual, nor is it peculiar to boarding schools.) Pierre was expelled.

He talked readily about his situation, but his sexual tendencies worried him a great deal; they were almost exclusively toward adolescents. He saw dimly that the boys who moved him were themselves very ambivalent, and that perhaps through them he was really seeking "the woman."

We began psychotherapy. At the time I was starting to undertake this myself with "well-motivated" clients who, for financial or other reasons, could not be referred to a therapist. Our sessions continued for about two years. Pierre left his half-hearted studies and the boarding-school environment in which he had nearly always lived. He got involved in a business he enjoyed, which made him travel all over France. Toward the end his therapy sessions were fewer and farther between, and yet something was happening.

One day he told me he had just had a striking dream. He was driving a van of some sort carrying several young men about his own age. He was upset because he had to cross the border, and he was not sure all his papers were in order. Now at the border everything went so smoothly that he found himself on the other side, rolling merrily along, while his pals had vanished into thin air. And the new world he discovered was filled with women.

The analysis of this dream was not carried too far, and I hardly ever saw the man again. But for several years he kept in touch by letter. A year after the last session he married. His relationship with his wife was excellent, and his work was equally suc-

cessful. The oldest of their children must be about twelve by
now.

Over the past twenty years, I have known at least three times
as many men as women with homosexual problems. Nearly all
my colleagues in medicine and psychotherapy report something
similar. It would be interesting, but difficult, to try to learn
why men seek help so much more often. The majority view seems
to be that the question of homosexuality is much more ambiguous
and changeable in women than in men. From a psychoanalytic
standpoint this makes sense.

Quite recently I had several sessions with a middle-aged woman from outside Paris. Like many of my clients, she came because she wanted to discuss her inner torment with a priest who
was also a psychologist.

Morphologically and physiologically, she was a perfectly normal woman. In her conservative clothes she struck me as not
very feminine, but clearly a female. Yet she had wanted to be
a man for as long as she could remember. Her self-image and
her sex were completely contradictory. Several years ago she
met a younger woman. I saw her friend twice; she was a bit of a
child-woman, but not in any flamboyant sense. Since they lived
some distance apart they met rather seldom, but they shared a
deep emotional bond. Their visits had erotic moments, which
concerned the women, yet they didn't really agonize over their
relationship.

This is just one example. I have seen married women in love
with female friends, two women living together with no overt
sexual relations, etc. Much more rarely I have seen the militant
woman of the suffragette or women's lib type; in these people, if
we are attuned to the unconscious, we often note deep-seated,
unrecognized distress.

There are other strange, tragic cases of contradiction between psychoaffective and physiological sex. The most striking example I have seen dates from about two years ago.

"Miss X" phoned to request a meeting; her voice seemed a bit odd. At the appointed time the doorbell rang and I answered it. There stood a tall, slender creature, in gaudy dress and heavily perfumed.

I showed her into my office, without comment, of course; we sat down and I listened. The change was startling. My client was a transvestite, as I had suspected from the start. He began to tell me about himself:

He was twenty-four, a nude dancer at a cabaret in the Pigalle district. Even as a young child he had wanted to be a girl; he had instinctively refused to act like a boy. The results were precocious transvestism, and many homosexual affairs of a passive type—and his job, as well.

Anatomically and biologically he was clearly male. He had even confirmed this by medical examination. He had taken hormone treatments to fill out his chest, and he was considering a sex-change operation to remove his male organs and replace them with a pseudovagina. It can be done, as we know. But it worried him from a religious standpoint. He was a Catholic, and had been raised alone by a pious and apparently neurotic mother.

On that score I said there was nothing to worry about, at least not in theory. In the deep contradiction of his identity, it did not strike me as immoral for him to seek a solution that would lead to a less tortured existence. The solution might seem shocking. But in his particular case it was not just a matter of castration, but a possible therapy.

From a psychological point of view, however, it was not so simple. Would this operation solve his problem, or complicate it? What would it mean to him in the long run? (In psychoanalytic terms, was this a wish for castration—or fear of castration?) Of

course the results could be positive, but nobody could predict
them with certainty. I thought it might help if he could gain some
insight into his own needs. I suggested he talk with an analyst
who could be "neutral" about the decision, neither encouraging
him nor trying to dissuade him.

It seems he was already thinking of this. He thanked me and
left, seeming less agitated. But I never saw him again, and I
don't know what he decided.

Over the years I knew two other men who were struggling
with the same basic problem. The first was about the same age,
and not very bright. He too "felt more woman than man."
Though he seldom wore women's clothes, he used makeup all
the time. He said he was waiting for his "Prince Charming" (a
virile man a bit older than himself, as I recall). At the age of
twelve, in 1945, he had been wounded during the liberation of
the Vosges and his right leg had had been amputated at the
thigh. But this loss did not seem to have affected his sexual
orientation, which had already been shaped in early childhood.

Nor did it now keep him from frequenting homosexual bars
and social gatherings. Equipped with a good artificial leg, and
often disguised as a woman, he would make the rounds hoping
to find his "prince." I don't know what happened to this man,
either. But he must have turned forty by now, and I don't imagine he is leading a very full life.

The second man, again in his mid-twenties, asked me to appeal on his behalf to the president of France; he wanted official
authorization to dress as a woman. He had been running into
impossible problems: for employment and social security he had
to appear as a male, and the frustration was more than he could
stand. (Of course I had no way to help him, having no political
connections whatsoever.)

This boy was a butcher, and his heavy, ruddy physique was
as far from feminine as could be imagined. Furthermore he had

no sex life at all, and hardly any desire. He masturbated on rare occasions, but that was all. He seemed perfectly normal physically, though since I saw him only once I could not verify this through an endocrinologist.

These three men and the middle-aged woman are torn in a strikingly similar way. There is a radical contradiction between their biological identity and the identity they live. As the saying goes, their skin doesn't fit them. But why not? And how can they be helped? These are strange questions.

Varied as they are, these stories are just a small sample of what I have heard and encountered through the years. Naturally the simplistic theories I started out with had to change. Then, as I got involved with clients through psychoanalysis, something else happened. I realized that my own affectivity was being challenged, mainly on an unconscious level. Why would I find this person sympathetic, even touching, while I could hardly tolerate some other one? Two incidents helped bring this awareness home to me.

When I first started doing psychotherapy, I agreed to a series of sessions with a man of about thirty. I hoped to prepare him for deeper, more systematic therapy with one of the analysts I knew. This client was not exclusively homosexual, but nearly so.

We got off to a good start. In fact, after a few weeks he told me that something inside seemed to be changing. He was feeling attracted, even physically, to a young woman he had met. Then one day he flatly told me: "I don't know if what we're doing is very useful. During the past few days it has dawned on me that I'm pretending to get well in order to please you." At least, that was the gist of what he said.

He was "pretending to get well." But in all honesty, because even he believed he was "getting well" until the day he saw what was happening.

Why did *I* have the desire that *he* "get well"? Suddenly the real question struck me. What was the basis of this desire in myself? At the time I found some good rationalizations. There was the "apostolic role": a doctor has the desire to cure his patient, using his own ideas and knowledge. But in this case was there a "patient" to "cure"? (We will return to this question in a more general sense.) My attitude had been quite natural, and at first glance quite legitimate. Yet it was clear that it had completely falsified the helping relationship he had wanted of me. There was also the idea, which traditional morality takes for granted, that it was "better" to be heterosexual than homosexual, and that it was my job to change him. (In a sense it *is* better, but not in *this* sense!)

But why him? For with other clients my "desire to cure" played a minor role. Why had I agreed to "take charge of him" —and not someone else? In the relationship that developed, he began trying to *please* me. That is he tried to satisfy the desire he perceived in me, but which was not recognized by either of us. I had certainly not thought there was any desire on my part. In this sense the relationship was fundamentally homosexual, and analysis was impossible because my own desires were mixed up in it.

So we ended our sessions, and I referred him to the other therapist. I learned through my colleague that he had, in fact, begun psychoanalysis. Since then I have had no news of him.

The issue remained, though, and raised questions I hardly suspected at the time. Around the same period another of my clients made a remark that really shocked me; it was an accusation that seemed to me totally unfair. It is only recently that I have been able to see the rightness of it, although I lost all contact with the man shortly after the incident.

He was about twenty, and came to me because of his homosexual tendencies and the conflicts they were causing him. I had

referred him to a psychotherapist I knew, and they were meeting regularly. But since we had friends in common, I continued
to see him from time to time. I was trying to convince him to
change, partly for "religious" reasons. On a day I remember
vividly he stormed out my door; his parting words were like a
slap in the face: "What arrogance!" I was stunned and hurt. I
was convinced what I had said was for his own good.

He was right. But I did not understand that until long afterwards. I was quite simply putting myself in the place of God.
I was acting as if I knew the "will of God" was that he become
heterosexual. Literally! And I was sure I was right. There, in
subtle disguise, is the cardinal sin of pride. The incident made
me question my own religious attitudes. What idea of God did
I have that I made myself his propagandist? (And not his apostle,
which is something different, maybe even opposite.) There was
only a distant, distorted relation to the gospel. I considered myself a Christian and a priest, yet I found myself on the side of
the "scribes and doctors of the Law." I was self-righteous, without
seeing that Christ was "somewhere else"—as in the scenes with
the Samaritan woman, with Simon the Pharisee, with the woman
taken in adultery.

I came to understand all this only gradually. But a crack had
been opened in my cultural wall of defense. In the years to come,
all the built-in standards—all the prejudices, in fact—that distorted my hearing were challenged radically by my growing
clinical experience. It is only recently that I have felt able to
formulate an approach which is somewhat new, or at least unconventional.

Especially in dealing with sexuality, our own emotions are
involved even if we won't admit it; any dogmatic preconceptions
may keep us from seeing what is really there. It is actually very
simple, but hard to accept. When observing reality we unconsciously focus on the facts which confirm our own hypotheses.

This problem is widespread. I have so often seen book reviews in which a critic reproached an author for not saying what he wanted to read, when he had not really "read" what the author wanted to say. This book will no doubt suffer the same fate.

I thus had to examine critically, one by one, my presuppositions on the homosexual question—all those ideas that once seemed so obvious. Here my faith and my clinical experience came together. I saw that such "doctrine" had very little to do either with the gospel or with reality.

Of course the Catholic doctrine is not the only kind that can block an observer's vision. We can see something quite comparable in the strange blend of psychoanalytical and Marxist notions that has been introduced by writers such as Marcuse and Reich. This "philosophy," in a parallel way, can make people deaf to human experience.

I would now like to present some ideas based on my own experience with homosexual men and women. I do not claim to offer a new doctrine of any kind, or to be exhaustive. I merely hope to encourage some serious thinking on the subject.

2. What Is the Question?

Homosexuality has existed in all times and all cultures. Of course we can't know much about life in the Vezere valley thirty or forty million years ago. I hardly think we have documentary evidence of the sexual problems of Cro-Magnon man. I also have no respect for theories some people develop on the basis of a few remnants of a civilization. Such "deductions" tell more about the fantasies and wishes of their authors than about the reality which cannot be explored.

Speaking for the historical period, though, we can say with near certainty: homosexuality has always existed among human beings. In different cultures it has been lived and identified in very different ways. In one place, homosexuality is punished by death. In another it is ignored. I recall my surprise one morning at the Saigon marketplace: two young men were intertwined, hands on each other's buttocks, while the crowd milled around them without noticing at all. In still another place, homosexuality is associated with some beneficent or ambivalent deity; it seems, for example, that this was the case with the people of Corinth whom St. Paul addresses. In any case, all these variations seem to reflect the different mythological and religious conceptions in each culture.

In human experience sexuality is the meeting place of life,

death, and love. Its challenge is so total and mysterious that it is no surprise that it is always closely associated with certain divinities, or with a mythic explanation of natural events. This is true whether or not the culture is "religious." The one profound exception is the Bible, where sexuality is not *directly* linked to transcendence. The homosexual question has always been placed in this context. Yet it is interpreted in such diverse ways that it poses special problems. Shouldn't all these mythic positions be viewed with caution?

Homosexuality is found only among human beings. This point must be clearly understood.

All studies of animals are conducted by human beings. We can put our observations into words, but only after they are colored by our unconscious emotional lives. In the last analysis we are talking about our own experiences. When we say, for instance, that a dog is "sad," in the strictest sense we don't really know what we're talking about. We translate his behavior into what he evokes in us—a feeling of sadness. If we acted like that dog, it would mean that we were sad. Actually we have no right to assume that the dog is sad.

What we can observe of domestic animals is in no way representative. They are too conditioned by human beings. Sometimes they are even caricatures; a certain cat's eczema may reflect the nervous anxiety of its master or mistress.

As for observing animals in the state of nature, it is a tricky business. If the animals in any way detect the presence of the human observer, it can affect their behavior. We cannot possibly avoid this problem.

There are signs among certain animals—especially mammals, it seems—of sexual activity between individuals of the same sex. But we cannot in any sense conclude that there are homosexual animals as such. This is simply, though mysteriously, because nothing in the human species happens exactly as in others. With humans there is always something other than instinct and conditioning to take into account. Animals are not homosexual any more than they are scrupulous, timid, dyslexic, or paranoid—at least not in the true sense of these words, which are based on projections of our own feelings.

I have to stress this point if we expect to get anywhere. It is naive, ridiculous, and unscientific to justify homosexuality by showing it is rooted in "nature" as reduced to animal biology. Gide does this in all sincerity. But then, what is there to justify? What insecurity is behind this argument? Not only is it not valid but, to make matters worse, this approach is ultimately misleading and depressing.

Attempts to divinize nature are always misleading. They can get us into contradictions from which we can't escape. We can follow Gide by thinking of "Nature" as some sort of Supreme Being; we can justify or condemn behavior according to her secret will. Then, however, we will have to condemn contraceptives which are "against nature." Some have gone so far as to say that the most natural way to fight the population explosion is through homosexuality. What is this nature goddess we have somehow inherited from Rousseau on which we base our fears as well as our unfounded security, and to which we so eagerly submit? It seems to me that whenever we look for "the meaning of the world," our investigations of nature only lead us up a blind alley.

Then again, it is depressing to be classed with the animals, even the "higher" ones. If the mother dog eats a few of her babies, or the praying mantis feeds on her mate during copulation, it is no reason for humans to do likewise. We often say that certain perverse behavior "reduces us to the level of the beasts." Yet it is exactly these perversions, sexual and otherwise, which do not exist among animals. The atrocities of war, for instance, are uniquely human. When we say that a person "acts like an animal," we are wrong. This is a defense mechanism we use to avoid seeing that such crimes are peculiar to human beings. They are peculiar to *us*. We usually harbor them in the form of unconscious wishes, but occasionally they break out into the field of our actions. The so-called dignity of man implies in itself that we can devise "horrible" things. It is thus regressive, false, and sterile to justify or to condemn homosexuality on the basis of animal behavior.

Let's think a bit more about this idea of nature. To a scientist the word refers to what happens when human will and actions do not intervene. It "comes of itself," and we merely observe it.

So when a homosexual says that his situation is "natural," he is right. He has done nothing to cause it; it has come of itself; he feels he was born that way, and that it is his nature. This is not the most common feeling among homosexuals, but we do find it. Only in the human species do things happen spontaneously —as far as the observer can tell. These things can cause problems, though: delusions, inhibitions, overcompensation, homocidal ideologies, heterosexual "quirks," homosexuality.

So what is "human nature" from a scientific point of view? It is what we observe, and try to understand. Thus it seems quite natural for human beings to behave in ways that are literally abnormal with respect to other species. We must realize that this poses a unique question.

The sexual organization of life is already apparent at the level of certain protozoans. In more complex organisms the sexual function becomes better defined and biologically more complex as well. But it is strictly a way of reproducing living creatures according to their own species. This is an aspect of the laws of invariance and teleonomy.

The human species seems much the same. The sexual function is still physiologically a means of reproduction, just as the digestive function, in all its complexity, keeps individuals alive. But while these physiological functions remain, in man there is an entirely new dimension, the sense of pleasure and of relationship.

In the case of digestion, this is all clear and nobody would question it—perhaps the subject is less dangerous. Animals eat. Humans have invented cuisine, beverages, the rituals of dining. Nothing could be less "natural." What cave man—or woman— dreamed of the idea of using the newly discovered fire to roast a chunk of reindeer meat, garnished with those plants that smelled so good in the nearby woods? Why? For pleasure. It was dangerous, though. You could be poisoned, especially if you added certain tasty-looking mushrooms. I believe it is extremely rare that an animal free of human influence, living in its natural habitat, is poisoned by "accident."

Over the years this risky discovery must have taken its toll in victims. But it was designed for pleasure—and for sharing pleasure as well. You would invite friends from the next cave and have fun together: "It tastes good, doesn't it?" Then you would bring on the mead, the wine, the whisky. Soon there must have been rituals of dining; they are certainly very old. Today, as well, dining is not just a matter of nourishment, for the food may not even be physiologically needed. Think of the snacks and hors d'oeuvres you eat without any hunger, just because it is good to eat together.

Then of course there is the other side of the coin. People can destroy themselves by overrefined, excessive, or misdirected tastes. They can bring on cirrhosis of the liver or hardening of the arteries, and die prematurely. Pleasure has its dangers, yet that doesn't make it worthless; after all, you can deliberately eat the deadly mushroom or take poison, if you simply want to die.

It is the same with the reproductive system. Human sexual activity and the search for pleasure are not limited, as in animals, to their physiological ends. To ensure the survival of the species, animals copulate. But humans "make love," a phrase which is not to be despised. It suggests making (building, inventing), and loving (which is nothing trivial). It can be important, for instance, for a couple to "make love" by putting reproduction aside for a while. They may need to deepen their own relationship, to build a secure home for their future children. This is the sense in which contraception is not "natural." It has been invented, and is thus artificial—but it is not "against nature."

In the light of these ideas, can we say that homosexuality is against nature? I don't think it is so simple. In one sense it is clearly true: homosexuality literally negates the physiological ends of sex (this is not the case when contraception is used as a means of family planning).

Yet there is still the other dimension, that of relationship and pleasure. We cannot assume that a relationship which is physiologically abnormal can never, in an emotional, sharing sense, be genuine. Just as we can't assume that a relationship which is physiologically normal will always involve real sharing. How many heterosexual relationships consist of "screwing," to use the vulgar yet quite accurate term, using one another instead of "making love."

Clearly I don't think we can get anywhere in our thinking if we stick to the categories of "with nature" and "against nature." This would be to ignore the complexity and conflict built into *human* nature.

The language that automatically comes to mind when speaking of homosexuality also calls for closer examination. We hear so many people say: "Homosexuals? Oh! They're sick!" Now it is clear that some homosexuals are sick. But we must not forget that there are also plenty of sick heterosexuals. My point is that the mere fact of having homosexual tendencies—though it may pose problems—is not "sickness" in the usual sense .

What do we really mean by sick? It is quite clear, of course, that we are dealing with a mental or nervous sickness, not with pneumonia or viral hepatitis. In current terminology someone who is sick suffers from a condition, acute or chronic, which interferes with living, working, loving, or having good relationships with other people. The condition can be self-induced, since people can make themselves sick. The qualification "mental" merely indicates a type—nonphysical—but there is no great difference in meaning.

If we look up *malade* ("a sick person") in Robert's dictionary, we find: "*malade*, 12th century. From the Latin *male habitus*, one who is in bad condition." This definition persists in the current sense of the word. A sick person is in a state which cuts him off to some degree from his usual activities and from his enjoyment of life. It is implied that this condition is not incurable; otherwise we would speak of permanent disability or terminal illness.

The word *maladie* ("sickness") is defined as "any organic or functional change which may be more or less serious and lasting." Bergson, in *The Two Sources of Morality and Religion*, writes: "But sickness is as normal as health. In fact, from one point of view, health is a continuing effort to prevent or avoid sickness." This reminds me of the quip: "Every healthy person is a sick one who doesn't know it." We are all potentially sick, and as another saying goes: "We recover from every sickness except the last one."

Clearly these categories cannot be applied to the homosexual state as such. Some people who have homosexual tendencies don't feel they are "in bad condition," and don't go looking for doctors to "cure" them. My impression is that they are not in the majority, but they do, undeniably, exist. That shows we must find other terms. They "have problems," as the saying goes, but do not in any way consider themselves sick.

On the other hand it is clear that a good many people whose tendencies are exclusively heterosexual *are* sick. Their problems may even be bound up with their sexual life; they may ask counselors to help "cure" their obsessions, perversions, inhibitions, etc.

I believe we must completely reject this vocabulary. It carries a built-in risk of what we might, by analogy, call "racism." To say that certain persons are "sick" makes a reassuring distinction: "*We* are healthy." What a misrepresentation!

Then again we hear about anomalies or abnormalities, which are not, in fact, synonyms. Many people who don't consider themselves "abnormal" still have the deep sense that "it is not normal to have these homosexual tendencies." I think this spontaneous distinction is very important.

The notion of anomaly is a matter of statistics. The radial artery follows a certain oblique path through the chest. In a few cases, however, this path happens to be different, further back or forward. This is an anomaly. The word has a purely statistical meaning, and does not imply sickness or deformity. In this sense it is clear that the homosexual condition is an anomaly: it is observed statistically in no more than 7 or 8 percent of the population. We do not need to bring in any note of qualitative judgment.

The notion of abnormality is different. What is normal conforms to a norm, or law. But what law are we talking about? Without getting into complicated issues, we can distinguish several different kinds of law.

First of all, there is what could be called the *law of society*. All civilization is based on a certain image of man and his relation to the world. What does not conform to this image is said to be abnormal. This law of society is normative, imperative. One must be "normal" to find a place in the culture in question.

This is a law in the moral sense, with notions of good and evil, of ostracism, guilt, etc. According to this purely cultural perspective, it is clear that homosexuality is judged by different norms from culure to culture.

In one place, such as Sparta, it is "normal" and does not pose any moral problems. In another it is rather seriously "abnormal" and condemned as evil; the more recent Western tradition is a good example. So according to the law of society the term normal is a relative one.

Another notion of law is implied by the phrase *the laws of science*. These norms, theoretically, at least, are no longer based on any particular society. The scientific method aims at objectivity by abstracting ideas from cultural data. The normative aspect of law totally disappears. We merely record what happens and how things relate to each other. Thus we can speak of the law of universal gravitation, which does not carry any moral implications.

Stating the law of gravity does not in any way suggest that people must obey it, or that it is morally wrong to want to come down from the Eiffel Tower without a parachute. The reference is not to morality at all. If man wants to conquer the law of gravity he knows that he can make use of another law, such as the law of density of gases, to invent the hot air balloon. What he is going to do with it is another question.

This area of scientific law includes the laws of growth and development of living creatures, teleonomy and invariance. A sperm and an egg unite. The fertilized egg travels through the tubes and attaches itself to the uterine wall. Something begins, a burst of endogenous development following a genetically predetermined plan. The first stage that can be observed from the outside is birth. A human being with unique structural characteristics emerges from the uterus. Now if the newborn arrives without a brain (anencephaly), or with hands directly connected to the shoulders (phocomelia), it is obviously not normal. That is, it does not conform to the scientific law of the development of the embryo. What happened? We don't really know, but we are starting to catch a few of the warning signals. The thalidomide tragedy taught us a great deal. In any case, whatever the mechanism may be, we can say this: something happened that prevented the free and complete development of the genetic potential built into the organism at the start. The notion of *abnormal* is forced upon us here; it does not, however, carry any moral implications at all. We are shocked to learn that the condition tends to be totally independent of anyone's will, and therefore no one is guilty. If the results are bad in the ontological sense (falling short of what should develop), they are certainly not morally bad (referring to sin or the punishment due to sin).

Freud pioneered the same kind of scientific approach to the uniquely human aspects of growth—psychic, affective, and sexual. He explored the potential for human relationships, which is suggested in the genetic code but develops according to its own laws.

In speaking of homosexuality we must exclude any reference to the law of society. We can then say that the homosexual condition—like many others—is abnormal in terms of the laws of science. Something happened that blocked the full development of sexual potential.

This is the process we must now consider.

3. The Other

Our emotional life has to be ambivalent. We relate both to people of our own sex and to people of the opposite sex; everyone, clearly, has sex. Why did it take so long for this basic fact to be recognized? And why is it still so often ignored? Each of us, therefore, has a built-in element which is homosexual —or let us call it homosexed to avoid discomfiting anyone.

A forty-year-old man and his thirty-eight-year-old wife have two children, a girl of twelve and a half and a boy of seventeen. Let's suppose these people really love one another—after all, it *does* happen! That means that each person feels something for the others: there may be affection, love, passion, and a whole range of conflicts as well. What the father feels for his son is clearly not identical to what he feels for his daughter; he loves him as a boy and her as a girl. The same is true in the case of the mother. The father's affection is "homosexual" toward his son and "heterosexual" toward his daughter. At least I hope so, for if he has no feelings toward his son, or loves him like a girl, I pity the poor boy!

Since birth, however, all sorts of things have happened to this man which allowed him to complete his own sexual development. The heterosexual urge was just a vague hint at first. Then it managed to take shape and develop unhindered until it found erotic expression. As a young man he fell in love with a woman who had followed a parallel course in her own sexual development. They entered into the exclusive but expansive relationship of marriage. Yet in a way I hope the man is still deeply "homosexual" when he talks to his son.

This development I have mentioned is hard to describe without being simplistic. But I must stress that all human affective and psychological growth is conditioned by the central fact of sexual duality—by the difference between the sexes. This difference is clearly not cultural; it is a biological given. Various cultures have handled it in various ways, but the question of sexual difference is universal. Judging from the violent reactions it can inspire, this question must be charged with deep, hidden anxiety.

The issue has been deftly stated in the form of a joke (maybe the humorists are more perceptive than the philosophers): "When the first living cell, upon reaching the age of puberty, saw that reproduction was just a matter of cutting itself in two, it was *bitterly disappointed.*" We are reminded of the myth of the original androgyne, which still leaves a trace in the story of Adam's rib in Genesis.

In short, throughout history this sexual dichotomy has been perceived as a disturbing rift. We look across a chasm with a feeling of vertigo, and we struggle to find a secure foothold in one or the other half of the species.

Since Freud's pioneering studies of the unconscious and of the emotional development of young children, we can better explain what is going on.[1] Each human being, in the course of a unique journey through a network of relationships, tends to find his or her satisfactory sex role. This role also tends to be satisfactory to other people; if not, the individual would feel trapped and un-

1. This passage is intended as a description, not as the last word on the "why" of things.

fulfilled. Humans have an innate drive prompting them to make this journey. We might say that each person has the urge to conquer that initial feeling of "vertigo" in response to the "other" who is "different." In fact sexual difference becomes the source of emotional security and potential relationship. In other words, most people eventually find their enjoyment in the other half of the species.

The word enjoyment is used deliberately. It means the growth of individual identity through the experience of pleasure and of relationship. Now pleasure in the Freudian sense is the resolution of a tension. It does not necessarily involve any actual orgasm, but refers to a general sense of euphoria which resolves (temporarily!) a state of tension. Pleasure is not restricted to the genitals.

The erotic and emotional sides of the personality do not always grow at the same pace. A teenage boy may be attracted to girls erotically long before he can cope with them emotionally. But in a very general sense, an adult male with homosexual tendencies shows that something in his personal history has kept him from gaining full access to the other as the source of enjoyment. I might note that a man who is exclusively heterosexual, but who runs compulsively to prostitutes, has also not found a satisfactory relation to the other.

Gaining access to the other is not to be viewed as the crossing of a frontier, as a total change of landscape at a given point in time (in spite of the symbolism of one of the cases cited in chapter 1). Today we know that it is gradual, conflict-ridden, even in a sense incomplete—like every aspect of the emotional life. Of course there are certain critical periods when life bursts into a new form. From a clinical point of view such terms as "puberty" serve as landmarks, and make communication possible. Yet from birth on, each person evolves through an absolutely unique course of events. His or her story cannot be equated with any other, even though there may be certain likenesses within a given culture.

A child is not born into a stereotyped situation, a world of ideological abstractions. It finds itself in a complex network of relationships among unique individuals. Plunged from the first into the dialectic of sexual duality, the child grows to find his or her own role. This process follows certain broad, common outlines, but is truly beyond classification.

Ordinarily each adult retains, deep down, traces of the archaic emotional and sexual stages of childhood and adolescence. Normally people live with such things without any great difficulties. But these unconscious vestiges can be brought to the surface in encounters with people who have problems with their own sexuality. This is not peculiar to homosexual problems. How does a family man respond to a friend who is known as a Don Juan, going from woman to woman because he cannot establish a real relationship?

Today, since Freud's ideas have passed into everyday language, most people have some familiarity with the stages of the emotional life. I don't want to review them here in any detail. But we should pause to consider what happens when a young child discovers sexual, anatomical difference. One doesn't have to be a psychoanalyst to see that the presence or absence of a "little peepee" is an urgent question for small children. We tend to laugh as we repeat such "childish words." Yet only from a psychoanalytic point of view can we get a sense of what this preoccupation means. Somehow, at a level which is almost completely unconscious, this preoccupation is at the very heart of the question of homosexuality. A childhood fear of the other has not been resolved. (The details, of course, vary from individual to individual.)

A six-year-old boy comes home one day from the local Catholic school. He is the only child of average middle-class parents who are neither prudish nor exhibitionist. He is bubbling over with a great discovery.

"Mommy! You know what? Today I learned how God created people!"

"Really?"

"First he made Adam. Then he was afraid Adam would get bored because he was all alone. So he took one of his ribs and made Eve. But there was this problem. He hadn't taken quite enough to make a little peepee. So he took a handful of hair and covered her up so she wouldn't notice what was missing."

This story is authentic. The boy in question must be about thirty now, and as far as I know his tendencies are exclusively heterosexual. I think his interpretation of Genesis is quite enlightening.

This family was not used to walking around the house naked. This is not necessarily preferable, and even suggests a trace of a taboo. So the boy's only image of the adult female came from watching his mother through the bathroom keyhole. Sexual curiosity is central—and it is all the more driving when not satisfied by the environment.

And yet this child saw the absence of a "little peepee" as something that should be hidden even from the interested party herself. Obviously it was a problem for him, and he imagined it would be equally painful for Eve to notice it. But what was this problem? Here the adult terms don't work because they are charged with feelings and cultural attitudes which are quite after the fact. Is it shame? A sense of inferiority? All we can say is that to the six-year-old boy, the absence of a penis in the female is an incompleteness; she must not learn about it, since she too would find it distressing.

The presence or absence of a penis is the crucial question for the child. It is associated with anxiety, even panic, in ways that vary according to whether or not the child actually has this organ. No doubt in different cultures people deal with the question differently, yet in some form or other it is universal. One example is the widespread occurrence of phallic cults: the male symbol tends to predominate because it is visible. To the primitive mentality—in children or in prescientific cultures—the absence of the phallus among women can only be perceived as an inexplicable lack.

Here is the whole dialectic of castration. When the child becomes aware of sexual differences—much earlier than most people think—this dialectic takes hold and demands some sort of resolution. This is the well-known stage of penis envy among girls, and fear of castration among boys "if they don't watch out." This response to the question of sexual difference seems to be native to the Greco-Roman West. But that is irrelevant. We are fixed concretely in this cultural tradition, and I can't see any point in imagining a different one, since it would no longer be ours.

So it all begins with a fear, which differs according to the sex of the child. Each boy and girl must somehow resolve it. The feeling of vertigo in the presence of the other tends to grow into desire, but the dizzying aspect never totally disappears. Then a discovery is made: the opposite sex is not just different, but complementary. The result is the temptation to become "one." Contact with the opposite sex—and not just in the genital sense—can seem to be the way back to the nostalgic myth of the original androgyne. The danger, though, is inherent in the sexual dialogue itself. Becoming one is a dangerous illusion; it removes the very basis of heterosexual relationships: the vertigo, the difference, the other.

Now certain very early emotional experiences may keep a child from getting beyond this primitive fear and finding his or her own sexual identity. I can't offer any textbook definitions, because the circumstances are unique to each individual. In any case, the child may be trapped at this stage, unable to gain free access to the other as source of enjoyment. One possible result is homosexuality—in the infinite variety I have been trying to suggest.

All unconscious affective life revolves around the phallus. It is a frightening symbol, a sign to the viewer of something missing. One of my clients told me how disturbed he was, as a boy, by a one-legged friend at boarding school who amused himself by playing with his wooden leg and making sick jokes. With homosexual men and women, in ways that are unconscious but somehow parallel, there is first of all a deep fear. Fear of the fellow creature who is radically other in terms of what is present or absent. Fear that something is missing (which is still just as strong as when the child first noticed that boys and girls were different). The archaic fear remains actual.

From this fear comes the preference for one who is "different but physically like me," and not "like me but physically different."

Over the last seven or eight years, I have worked with some fellow doctors and psychiatrists on a study of sexuality. We gathered information from classes of eleven- and thirteen-year-old pupils at a large boys' school outside Paris. They had not yet been exposed to formal sex education.

We noticed that one pattern kept recurring, though we have just recently started wondering why. With the eleven-year-olds we would present the basic facts of anatomy, physiology, and biology; then we would respond to a barrage of questions. To encourage free communication we were each alone with the boys, without anyone who might represent the powers that be. One of the very first questions was always: "What are twins?"

We didn't pay much attention to this. But years later we were still being asked the same thing. What could this insistent question mean? We felt that the most likely hypothesis was linked to the disturbing problem of the "double." Each child was trying to grow more conscious of his own identity by referring to an imaginary double, a figure that must be based on the mirror image. The boys were interested mainly in the question of identical twins; these twins are always of the same sex, and each is simultaneously identical and different. The imaginary double is both attractive and disturbing; it reassures us like a reflection, but suggests a kind of alienation as well.

When we held the same kind of sessions with boys who were two years older, one of the questions that always came up was, in fact, about homosexuality. We did not think this was simply because the problem is being discussed openly these days, but because it was a very real preoccupation. It seemed to be part of the normal search for individual and sexual identity: the need to be alone to be oneself. Here again was the question of the double, in its next stage. Most of these boys, facing the crisis of their own adolescence, were seeking to reassure themselves through a nostalgia for the double. Homosexual friendships, which may be emotional or erotic, are quite common at this time. This is especially true in the single-sex groups that teenagers themselves seem to prefer. Even when the child's growth toward the other has been normal and free up to this point, there is still a kind of fear or anxiety to deal with. There is still some of that childish uncertainty about sexual identity and about the solitude of the self. All of this is revived by the crisis of puberty. Here is the root of the boys' questions. By talking about the problem, by getting to understand it (assuming, of course, that someone would answer their questions), the boys were trying to free themselves from the imaginary double lurking in their unconscious.

What made the situation delicate was that our audience must

have included some boys whose own journey to the other had long ago been stopped, and whose personalities were truly homosexual. We had to avoid complicating their lives with guilt feelings or panic, while still answering the questions from the group. We felt that we managed to do it. The boys also knew that two or three times a year we would make ourselves available to anyone who wanted to talk with us.

The data from our informants reminds me of some lines by Alfred de Musset: "A young man dressed in black/ Who resembled me like a brother." There again is the specter of the double. Why "dressed in black?" De Musset's relations with women don't seem to have been the best. But that is another question, and it would be ridiculous to try to psychoanalyze him on paper.

The important point is that this relationship with the double is clearly by its very nature homosexual. The more a boy can free himself from the unconscious presence of his double, the more he can accede to the full enjoyment of the other, and the less likely it is that he will become homosexual. This interpretation may sound a bit too pat, but in my experience it fits the facts.

I recall in this connection a conversation with a thirty-year-old doctor. His marriage, children, and career were really flourishing. Yet at times he felt shaken, even a bit erotically, to meet a man about his own age bearing his own first name. (The name in question is not especially common today.) Not everybody by that name had this effect on him; only those who, for some impalpable reasons, touched off the problem of the double.

A popular expression explains this very well: the "alter ego"; "another self." People can hardly find anything better to say of a great friendship. In fact, though, the phrase is highly ambivalent. The other is not completely other, since he is myself; yet he is not really myself since he is other. If we are not careful we will find ourselves back in the stage of the mirror, in a homosexual relationship with the double. It is odd that to speak of friendship we use an expression which, taken literally, suggests the depths of narcissism. By contrast I think of the words of Montaigne, when asked why he and La Boétie were friends: "Because he was himself, and I was myself." There all is clear and each is in his own place. I might add that this was a normal "homosexed" relationship.

The term *narcissism* has entered the picture, and it is no accident. The myth of Narcissus aptly expresses the vertigo of attraction to the double. The young hero looks at his image in the waters of a fountain, and falls in love. As if he couldn't leave this image of himself facing him, and get beyond the jubilation of the baby who first recognizes himself in the mirror. As if he were afraid to look too soon at anything else. Too soon, that is, before reaching the fullness of his own inner identity. Too soon to face the other, the nymph Echo, the woman. And the myth, in a poetic but terribly cruel way, shows that this blockage is regressive. Narcissus is changed into a flower; though beautiful, it is also the sign of a vegetative life. And his sexual symbol, the daffodils, are the sexual organs of plants.

Narcissus, held back by some nostalgia for himself, cannot gain access to the enjoyment of the other who is different. This is the deep meaning of the myth; it is the question of homosexuality in the broadest sense of the term.

There are many clinical examples of people who, psychologically, are in just the position of the mythic hero. They are attracted by people of the same sex who are like their own narcissistic reflection. Sometimes the image is reversed: a little dark-haired boy is attracted to big blond fellows who are what he would like to be; it is a bewildered and hopeless quest. Others are attracted to young men who resemble them directly. This resemblance may be physical, but very often it is spiritual. This poses another question: is a relationship possible if the otherness is recognized? But that isn't easy, since it is precisely the element of "difference" which is lacking from the start.

I believe that this problem of narcissism is central to the psychological makeup of people with homosexual tendencies. It appears, of course, in very diverse forms. To one man or woman, it may be associated with the idealized image of a father or mother. This remains a deeply narcissistic projection, since the element of difference is not there. Men who have not been able to resolve their Oedipal crisis are a classic example. Totally unable to deal with the other, they are emotionally dependent on their mothers and sexually engaged in a never-ending search for a double. This double may even be projected in the form of a virile yet loving father whom they never had.

In heterosexual relationships (both emotional and erotic), sexual difference is clearly the basis of the encounter. Each of the individuals can find enjoyment in the other. I don't mean that this is always what happens. There are heterosexual couples who are very narcissistic, despite surface appearances. Yet the possibility of confronting the other still exists.

In homosexual relationships it is precisely the other who has been driven away by all kinds of unconscious forces, especially fear. Homosexual desire itself is rooted in the aggravation of an already painful narcissism. The homosexual encounter is the doomed confrontation of two narcissistic personalities.

Though some readers will object, I believe that the homosexual couple is a practical impossibility. But we must agree on terms. The word *couple* tends to be ambiguous. In Robert's dictionary the first definition is: "Two things of the same species which happen to be taken or considered together." Thus we say a "couple" of cows when we are only thinking of the number, but a "pair" when we mean two animals who live and work together. Two pals get along famously, always playing pranks and causing trouble; people say, "They're quite a pair!" without even thinking of the word couple. Yet in current usage, couple has taken on a special meaning. It refers to a lasting union formed by two creatures of the same species—human—but different and complementary in sex. By this very fact, the union tends to bring forth a third creature, who is different from the other two, but takes after them in many ways including sexuality. This tendency exists whether the third is wanted, prevented, or desired in vain.

In speaking of a homosexual relationship the term *couple* is thus not suitable; *pair* fits better. We would say, "a pair of friends." The current meaning of *couple* is based on sexual difference and the possibility of fertility. On the other hand, the homosexual relationship is based on the impossibility of dealing with the other. So I hope my readers will go along with the word *pair*. I will use it as a step toward a more accurate vocabulary, and certainly not as any kind of value judgment. This latter point strikes me as crucial.

Homosexuality is shaped by narcissism and by the haunting image of the double. The lasting homosexual pair, who grow together in a positive way, is a rare phenomenon. Clinical experience shows that disillusionment and tragic breakups are the rule. The heterosexual couple can work, for the two of them and for their children; it happens more often in real life than in literature. The homosexual pair in essence cannot work and finds itself at an impasse. There are exceptions; I have known several of them. Yet they seem to be the exceptions that prove the rule. For the most part, the narcissistic element in homosexuality is too strong for a lasting pair to evolve.

The counselor working with homosexuals faces serious problems in such situations. It hurts to see a client standing on the brink, basing his hopes on what is clearly an illusion. When that illusion fades, how will he endure the trauma? I have known

cases of suicide. Yet the truth is that most people survive breakups better than might be expected.

It is often very hard for exclusively homosexual men and women to accept the impossibility of having children. This is especially true for men. After all, a woman can always "make a baby"
if she wants to, though it does not strike me as boding very well
for the child in question.

I remember something I heard one evening fifteen years ago.
Hoping to gain some understanding, I had joined the crowd of
men at a music hall lounge known as a meeting place for homosexuals. I found the scene surprising and rather sad. Right near
me a charming, quite affected young man was telling his com-
panion that he had to leave. "I'm going to find Jacques. Good
night. Or maybe I'll get a little one!" I still recall that flippant
line. What despair, what suffering, was it masking?

Most of the breakups are caused by the driving possessiveness
in which the homosexual tendency is rooted. It is the possession
and rejection of the double who cannot be reached. Yet we can
see real devotion, even self-sacrifice, among homosexuals. Often
this is only a passing element, and soon the bitterness wells up
again. But can't all this be just an exaggeration of the ambivalence which shapes all human relationships? In most cases the
other is not exactly what we might wish.

Sometimes, though, a relationship may be passionate at first,
then grow into something else. The two become what we would
call a pair of friends. This is far from common, but it does happen. So far as I can tell, it occurs more often among women. I will
describe two situations.

The first is based on a clinical example from chapter 1. An exclusively homosexual man falls in love. The one he loves is
heterosexual, but likes him as he would any male friend. Quite
deliberately, out of love, in fact, the first man renounces not
only any erotic fulfillment of his own desires, but even the deep-

rooted possessiveness that might lead him to take control of his friend's life. I had many conversations with a man who did this. I grew to understand what suffering this could bring him—but also what richness. He was able to establish a deep and quite stable friendship with the other man and with his family. The friend knew what was going on, and his wife, with keen sensitivity, no doubt understood everything. I felt this transformation had been made possible by the human strengths of the man in question, and especially by those of the friend and his wife.

I have observed the second situation a few times. Two homosexual men fall in love and start living together. Little by little the relationship is transformed and becomes less passionate. There are quarrels, jealousies, scenes, and infidelities. But a real friendship is established and each fears solitude too much to consider a separation. So they go on living together, supporting each other in a life which doesn't always run smoothly. The erotic element fades or disappears. Each man has his passing affairs, which are more or less tolerated by the other. I knew a pair of this sort formed by a man in his forties who had been seriously handicapped as the result of an accident, and a younger man of about thirty who was very devoted to him. I don't know how long the relationship lasted. But I suspect that the older man, especially in view of his handicap, was too possessive for the pair to survive indefinitely. Note, however, that such unstable, possessive relationships are also found among heterosexuals who are immature or neurotic. And traces of the problem are common to most marriages in our culture.

The chorus of a drinking song is significant:

> Here's to you, Étienne, here's to you, old pal!
> Without these bitches we would all be brothers.
> Here's to you, Étienne, here's to you, old pal!
> Without these bitches we would all be happy.

When men get together and sing over dessert, the most faithful and loving husband sings as loud as the fickle or the cuckold. Are they just letting off steam? Why?

Then there are the words of the marching song: "If you don't want your wife to bug you, don't get married!" It's odd, but I don't think women get together to sing their own version: "If you don't want your man to bug you . . ." In our culture, women are more discreet.

It is *abnormal* (in the scientific sense of the term) to have homosexual tendencies. Something happened which cuts some people off from the enjoyment of the other sex. But just what sort of thing happened? Is it organic? Psychological?

This question does not come from any sociological authorities who want to impose some preconceived pattern of sexual behavior on everybody. It comes from the frequent, explicit requests of people who are dissatisfied with their own situation. I stress this point because a small minority of homosexuals would like to impose Reich's sociological alibi: homosexuals are fine; society is perverse. Those who swallow such theories may be disturbed in more areas than sex. I recall that before a conference on homosexual problems, letters and phone calls threatened me with the worst reprisals if I attended, and warned of "commandos." Now most of the participants I got to know at the conference were miles away from wanting to impose anything on anybody. A few did, I must admit, but we will come back to them. One Canadian woman wrote me vehemently, stating that people had no right to "cure homosexuals." I replied flatly that it was not a question of curing, but of knowing what to say to the many people who asked us for help. I didn't feel she had the right to stop these good people from coming to see us, or us from listening to them. In short, I said I couldn't stand the idea of any dictatorship, including that of the self-styled homosexual revolutionaries.

That means that to understand what causes an individual to have homosexual tendencies, we must renounce all dogmatism, and especially all attempts to reduce the facts to a simple, definitive, categorical explanation. Otherwise we suggest that we know something definite and want some power over others which would compromise individual liberty. All in all, the problem is quite analogous to many other life problems: scruples, inhibitions, obsessions, shyness, etc.

I deliberately will not provide a bibliography or a rehash of scholarship on homosexuality. Numerous books, articles, and laws have appeared. I have read many of them, and discussed them with friends and with colleagues who work with the problem. But since I am not teaching a course, I will not cite required reading—if only to avoid making biased choices.

All these life problems, including homosexuality, go back to the earliest years of life. Are they organically determined, or are they rooted in affective experience? Is it organicism in the tradition of nineteenth-century scientific thought, or psychogenecism, an awkward name for theories based on the work of Freud?

The organic dimension has two aspects: genetic and hormonal. Perhaps the homosexual tendency is written in the genetic code, in the chromosomes; the criminal tendency could be written in the same way. Or perhaps the homosexual tendency results from some hormonal imbalance; some years back there was a lot of talk about the 17-ketosteroids.

The psychological dimension is the life history of individuals. This includes their relationships since birth with those around them; and even before birth, in the way they were experienced in the minds of those who awaited or dreaded their arrival. This is the field of knowledge explored by psychoanalysis.

It should be noted that there is no way to tell the exact role of genetic heritage in the life of any human being. It is obvious that some genetic component exists. But what is it, and how much does it shape the course of human development? We cannot possibly know. Right from the start, affective and cultural influences come into the picture, forming the unique history of the individual. The structure of the human brain differs from that of animals in that it includes (following a cybernetic model) an organizing sector. This is the orbital-frontal lobe, which serves no physiological purpose, and which to a large extent is not programmed in advance. It is the life story of the individual which programs it progressively from birth on.

Returning to our original question, there has never been any proof that the homosexual tendency is part of a person's initial genetic makeup. Tempting hypotheses of this sort have always been belied by some fact or other. I will cite just one striking case. Twins were born into a family. They were identical twins, with the same genetic makeup. At the age of twenty-two, one of them was homosexual, and tormented; the other had no sexual problems and was already forming just the right love relationship with the woman he eventually married. But these twins, for complicated reasons, had been separated from birth. One had been raised by his parents, the other by his grandparents. They didn't start living together with their parents until they were twelve or thirteen years old.

We need just one case of this sort to shatter any illusion of an exclusively genetic explanation of the homosexual tendency. The only difference between these two boys was their affective history since birth. It would seem more logical to look in this direction for some explanation of their contrasting development.

There is also absolutely no proof that the homosexual tendency is linked to any hormonal imbalance. For many years the same process has been repeated: some writer has found the hormonal

explanation of homosexuality—until the day someone else dis-
proves it through clinical evidence. The hormonal imbalance in
question is found among people with no homosexual problems,
while actual homosexuals show no hormonal disturbance at all.

There are undoubtedly some men who are morphologically
very effeminate and some women who are mannish. These characteristics may even coincide with homosexual tendencies, in
which case it is tempting to think that the problems result
from something organic. Yet we can find people who are
morphologically ambiguous—even in voice—whose tendencies
are exclusively heterosexual. At the same time, we very often see
homosexuals whose morphology is entirely normal. A certain
young man talks like a girl, and walks with a sensuous, simpering
gait. He is playing a role, most often without consciously trying,
and even in spite of himself; he is a caricature of a woman. If we
watch him, we soon see that he is acting and exaggerating. A
physiological and hormonal examination shows that he is completely normal. Something else must be going on.

We find an extreme version of this puzzle among the *trans-
sexuals*. I have seen a number of them, and not one had any
trouble at the somatic level. One of them was really a handsome
fellow. He was a dancer at a "gay bar," but if you saw him during a medical exam you would wonder by what feat of mimicry
he managed to appear feminine. Of course, those who patronized
the night club must have been psychologically prepared to accept him.

Even in the very rare situations when something physical is
clearly the basis of a problem, we must ask how this problem
relates to the behavior. I have seen several cases of serious genital malformation: pseudohermaphrodism from embryonic atro-
phy of the genital tract; sex error from birth due to the same
cause; morphologic ambiguity due to the "feminine testicle." Let

me repeat that these are all *very* rare. Yet in the people I saw, it seemed that the libido and sexual behavior were influenced at least as much by psychogenic factors (both affective and cultural) as by the physical problem, however grave.

We can draw one conclusion. Some people suffer from their homosexual tendencies—I believe they are in the majority. If they consciously wish for heterosexuality, and really want to move in that direction, the only route that can possibly get them there is psychotherapy. I have never seen the slightest lasting change of this sort from so-called hormone treatments. Is it perhaps because this kind of therapeutic relationship is based on a false notion of sickness? On the other hand, the only people I have known who achieved a real and lasting evolution did so via a rather long psychoanalytic journey which they had freely undertaken. I have already described several cases. They formed helping relationships with true counselor-analysts[2]—people who, because they have struggled and come to know their own affectivity, do not let their desires get mixed up with the work of their clients. Only then can the person know any meaningful transference, self-analysis, and—sometimes—the release from archaic fears and repression.

I can't illustrate this process with a clinical example. It would take volumes to record a history which may unfold over a period of years, and which means reliving and trying to resolve conflicts which have long been buried. All I can do is point out the facts: the uselessness of hormone treatments, which may even complicate matters; the established successes of true analytic relationships; yet the very low incidence of these successes. On the latter

2. There are some therapists, doctors and even psychiatrists, who do psychoanalysis after reading Freud. The advice they give, for they do, ironically, give it, makes me wonder about their own psychological balance.

score, perhaps the obstacles that keep these people from reaching the other are often encountered too early in life to be brought to light now. In any case, over the past twenty years I have become convinced that psychological factors are much more basic to homosexuality than organic factors. As I see it, the proof is that only psychotherapy can help even a few people to change.

This poses a more general question which has never fully been answered. Psychoanalysis is a matter of relations and words, with no physical or chemical agents. By what mechanism, in neurological terms, can it influence the physiological and microchemical reactions of the brain? I don't believe we know at all; we can only affirm that it happens, and catch a glimpse of the affective route that is followed. All we can say, in terms of cerebral cybernetics, is that the orbital-frontal organizer is not fully and finally programmed, even in adults. Something happens that is not merely electronic.

And it is also not simply conditioning. Of course conditioned reflexes play a large part in our behavior. Yet even habits involve an affective area that cannot be reduced to simple training. The proof is that we can change our habits, for well-considered reasons, but also through emotional growth. In the case of homosexuality, any change that occurs through counseling is obviously not of a rational order; we do not reason a person into changing his or her sexual orientation. But it seems just as clear that the change goes deeper than the level of conditioned reflexes. In this sense, the problem is like that of detoxification. We know that behavior modification does not cure alcohol or tobacco addiction unless people are personally motivated—unless they first, of themselves, question their way of life.

From time to time psychiatrists or doctors claim to have solved the problem. They publicize a new treatment for homosexuality, whether in the form of chemotherapy or of behavior modification. There is usually considerable interest among certain homosexuals. This is understandable, for such an idea rests on the assumption that homosexuality is an illness, in the same class as leukemia or tuberculosis. But this is false, as we have seen; the question is wrong from the start.

Most important, I feel, it is an error of scientific method to reduce human problems to the biological or neurological level. This is not by any means limited to the problem of homosexuality. All too often this line of thinking goes along with a harsh rejection of Freudian insights and their possible usefulness.

Why? No doubt because according to Freud, the therapist no longer has any preconceived knowledge, and is no longer in charge of things. This is a real reversal of attitude, leading away from what could be called the domination—even the dictatorship—of medicine. Until I was a surgeon of almost thirty, I myself had no contact with clinical psychology. So I think I know how hard it is to change, but also how essential if we want to be able to help those who come to us.

Otherwise we can get people into worse trouble than ever. I have seen it happen, unfortunately. A homosexual man in his thirties consults a doctor whose point of view is foreign to psychoanalysis, even "anti-Freudian." By this very attitude, the doctor claims to have some prior knowledge of what is causing his client's problems. At the same time, the client finds himself facing the "One Who Knows." Let's recall that the root of the problem is in the client's archaic personal history. That means the doctor actually knows nothing, while the client does not know what he knows. The doctor then proceeds to take charge of the affair, and in accord with his illusion of knowing, prescribes some treatment—hormones, behavior modification, psychotropic medicines. Between the two of them is formed a truly homosexual active-passive relationship, where there is no more space for thinking. And since the knowledge is illusory, anything can happen, even a temporary semblance of cure whose aftermath may be catastrophic.

The physician gives advice. There are doctor's orders, urgent directives which set certain conditions: "If you do not do this or that I guarantee nothing." Of course! The conditions refer to that knowledge the doctor supposedly has. The advice I have heard most often is to go to a well-chosen prostitute, or to get married. Incredible as it may sound, there are still doctors, even psychiatrists, who give this sort of advice.

It doesn't take much thinking to see the gross inanity of the former suggestion. Pushing a boy who feels no physical attraction to women into the bed of a prostitute—even a "well-chosen" one—is courting disaster. He is going to prove to himself that he is even more homosexual than he thought, and to prove it to the doctor as well. The image of woman he gains from his escapade is not about to overcome his archaic fear of the other; it can only send him back to his dim narcissistic specters. Also I admit I am disgusted to see a doctor (even a so-called Catholic!) prescribe a prostitute—a human being—to be taken like a spoonful of medicine. I don't think I have ever known a woman doctor to give this sort of advice. It's strange. This happens between men: the male doctor sends his male client into a situation where the female does not truly and palpably exist as a person. So there is a homosexual relationship between the two men. This raises questions about how the doctor deals with the homosexual elements in his own unconscious, regardless of how his marital and family life may appear.

As for the advice to marry, it is based on the same psychological error as the referral to prostitutes. Only now there is the additional prospect of a life together that may be a living hell. Here again the woman is reduced to the level of a medical solution, like insulin for diabetes, or gardenal for epilepsy. I think

that here, too, it is male doctors who give such advice; or I suppose it could come from a female doctor who was herself homosexual or sadistic.

I have also known a few doctors who react in a "moral-indig-
nant-authoritarian" style. This leads them to a strange contradiction. They were horrified by the Nazi doctors who sterilized
Jews, gypsies, and political deviants; yet they are ready to castrate, by force if necessary, certain homosexuals who threaten
public order. The idea can still come up in connection with
some man who compulsively roams the public toilets, making
propositions to anyone and everyone, and is nabbed once or
twice a year by the police: "It might be doing everybody a
favor . . ." But first of all, it would be naive and simplistic to
think that anything would be changed; the obsession is not
located in the sexual organs. Then too, what impact can such an
operation have on the psyche of the person in question? When
it is a matter of sex change (genetically a fiction, but perhaps
warranted in some cases of transsexualism), we might give it a
second look. But castration to "neuter" is a sobering idea.

What do they want, these doctor-dictators who are ready to
castrate others to make them conform to their views? Doctors,
too, have their unconscious, as I am well aware.

Now the fact is that many people go to talk with someone
about their homosexual tendencies, just as other people go to
talk about their heterosexual problems. If a man goes to the doctor because his belly aches, it is simple enough. Examination,
diagnosis: it's appendicitis. The doctor operates and removes an
appendix that is red and full of pus; two weeks later there is no
problem to speak of.

But homosexuality is different. There is nothing to remove
(except in the fantasies of the doctor-castrators). What is making the client suffer is not somatic. Then again, the doctor no
longer has any power over the problem. A person may freely

enter into a helping relationship with a counselor—but this is not the same at all. On the basis of twenty years' experience, I believe it is a grave mistake to confuse these two situations.

We will return to the question of the helping relationship. In concluding this chapter I just want to stress one point: to regard homosexual life problems as an illness over which we can exert power is a scientific aberration.

4. Homosexuality and Society

Cultural Differences

Throughout the world, there are still cultural groups who think of intercourse as a magical act: the man and woman perform a sort of ritual which catches them up intensely, but briefly. Then, if the divinity is pleased, she grants them a child.

On the other hand, a couple who knows something about the activities of eggs and sperms perform the identical sex act with an entirely different meaning. There are occasional lapses in the form of such pious expressions as "God has blessed our union." But they know, at least implicitly, that the divinity has no direct influence on fertilization.

So far as we know, homosexuality has existed in all times and in all places. What changes from culture to culture is the way people interpret it. It would be interesting to explore the place of homosexuality in various societies throughout history, and to do a comparative study. But it would be quite an enterprise; then again, the conclusions could not help but be debatable, if not suspect. As a European of 1974, I could only get an idea of the Hittite culture of the second millennium B.C., and this would be only my idea. Of course there are documents, but there is also interpretation and imaginative projection on the part of the observer. I will consider here just three "cultures" which are more familiar to us; yet this sort of study is also not beyond criticism.

Greek Culture

People often speak of "Greek love." They mean the homosexuality of Socrates and Plato, which was quite different, it seems, from what happened in Sparta. But what do we really know about all this? Is what we know from the *Symposium* and from the Platonic tradition representative of Greek culture as a whole? Isn't it more likely a view of a very limited segment of the population, of a "school"?

Plutarch, for instance, did not agree at all on the privileged status of homosexual love. We know very little about the everyday customs of the average citizens of Athens. There is no evidence that they thought and lived like the little group of intellectuals who surrounded Socrates and Plato. Imagine an ethnologist of the year 3000 who is studying French customs from 1950 to 1980. He would make a big mistake if he thought they were accurately shown in traces of the aesthetic-pornographic theater of the times, or in the more or less intellectual literature of Saint-Germain-des-Prés.

We would be just as mistaken to see Greek culture through one literary and philosophical tradition. This approach would provide an ideal screen on which to project phantasms, and there are those who are eager to paint Greek love in idyllic colors. If a time machine out of H. G. Wells could drop them in ancient Athens, they might be disillusioned by the prosaic and at times sordid reality.

Greek love seems to have been mainly pederasty, in the etymological sense of the term: the attraction of adult males toward adolescents. Pederasty, for a tiny clique, was the route to the most profound philosophical thought. Yet it was not really homosexuality in today's clinical sense. It's strange; amid all the foggy notions about Greek love, very little is said about Aristotle. Is it because he didn't share the same inclinations? But that is beside the point. It would be as foolish to argue anti-pederasty by citing Aristotle as to argue pro-pederasty by citing Socrates. Despite differences between Athens and Sparta, we do know that Greek civilization as a whole did not attach any real importance to women. Roman civilization before its decline had a higher regard for women, and for marriage. But Greece, whether in war or in the arts, strikes us as dominantly masculine. The question of sexual difference was evaded, while homosexuality and "educational pederasty" hadn't much competition. At least, this is how it looks from our vantage point.

No doubt things were very different in the wider Greek world far from Athens. I think of the people of Corinth as St. Paul knew them at the start of the Christian era. Sects and initiation cults were multiplying, brought from the Orient and combined to some degree with Greek culture; the result was probably a great deal of confusion and disorientation. Many of these sects viewed sexual activity as a sort of communion with the gods. It is in this context that we must read the letters of Paul: he warns that this God whom he preaches about and whom he knows through Jesus Christ completely transcends orgasm. He simply reminds us to keep things straight.

Islam in North Africa

When I visited Fez in 1952, I was in for some surprises. I went with a doctor who was very pro-Arab and pro-Moslem, and who knew the area thoroughly. For the first time I realized how much Islamic religion is like the Judaism of the Old Testament.

In terms of our subject, I learned many new things about Moslem sexual mores. The university students I met in Morocco carried on homosexual relationships openly and as a matter of course, yet this did not keep them from marrying and finding their place in society after graduation. I don't know, however, if this pattern still occurs today.

As far as I could tell, it was essentially a matter of a somewhat prolonged period of adolescent behavior. This was supported by the atmosphere of single-sex boarding schools, and most likely by the cultural conception of marriage as well. Yet according to my colleague the percentage of truly homosexual adults was probably no greater than in Europe.

It should be noted that in the Islamic world as a whole, a woman's place is not equal to that of a man. This is in keeping with the norms of a polygamous society where, more so than in a monogamous culture, a woman is considered an object of comfort, pleasure, or wealth—or else a good breeder. With few exceptions, she has no say in running things. On this score, could the Islamic world be analogous to ancient Greece? In both cases the popular mentality does not really assume that the other is equal. Things seem to be changing, though—perhaps in Tunisia and Algeria more so than in Morocco.

There does seem to be a strong element of homosexuality among the Islamic people, but it is not necessarily expressed in any genital or erotic sense. It pervades the cultures and psychological attitudes of North Africa. It may seem trivial, yet it is significant that we see crowds of men—but few couples—in the public squares.

Hebrew Culture

The biblical documents as a whole, from Genesis to Revelation, form a singularly rich cultural achievement. Yet there are few detailed descriptions of customs in the sense that a modern historian might expect. There is little to give us a concrete sense of how the Hebrews actually lived. By contrast, almost every detail helps us to understand—or to misunderstand! —how they thought of the world, humanity, and the great questions of existence.

In terms of sexuality, the central theme is contrast, or even contradiction. On one hand the couple is the very foundation of the world: the interpersonal couple joined in mutual acceptance. Man and woman take each other in equality as well as otherness, in total and permanent fidelity—through an inner existential need, not through any outer force of law. Yet on the other hand sexuality is mysterious, as we see in the mythic language of Genesis 3; conflict and tragedy are so basic to life that the couple never fully succeeds. All these themes mingle with the ancient cultural roots of Near Eastern nomadic tribes. Polygamy and divorce are condoned in practice, though totally contrary to the ideal which is set forth. The history of the people and their kings is filled with marital disasters. Even the genealogy of Jesus of Nazareth includes at least two flagrant cases of adultery, one amid especially shocking circumstances (David and Bathsheba).

How does the Bible deal with sexual orientations? It is enlightening to compare two texts: the story of the friendship of David and Jonathan, and that uniquely powerful collection of poetry, the Song of Songs.

The relationship of David and Jonathan is described in 1 Samuel 18–31 and in 2 Samuel 1. In these passages, the reader is first of all struck by the violence of the times. We get an impression of merciless battles among tribes and clans struggling for the dominant power that would bring some unity. The situation strongly resembles the bloody battles which transformed the feudal mosaic and led to the monarchy of seventeenth-century France. From this standpoint, David and his son Solomon are in the roles of Richelieu and Louis XIV.[1]

It was in this seething, barbarous context that David and Jonathan met. This was around the end of the second millennium B.C. Saul, the first king, had managed to assume a shaky control with the support of the prophet Samuel, though Samuel himself remained uneasy about the very principle of the monarchy. The kingdom was at war with the original occupants of the area, the Philistines, Amalekites, and others. In spite of the brave deeds of the king's son Jonathan, the war was going badly. David was the youngest son of a Bethlehem stock breeder; in the story he also appears as a man of war and a musician. Of course it would be a mistake to read the historical books of the Bible like the works of modern historians. The narratives were compiled three or four centuries after the events, and it may be hard to find the historical fact on which an elaborate legend is based. Was Goliath really ten feet tall?

On two occasions we are told that David was handsome, "with fine eyes and pleasant bearing," that he was "prudent in speech, a man of presence," and that Yahweh was with him. From the start he charmed Saul, and with his lyre he calmed the king's spells of depression. From their first meeting, something passed between Jonathan the king's son, and David. "Jonathan's soul became closely bound to David's and Jonathan came to love him as his own soul." They were no doubt about the same age, hardly out of adolescence. We can't help thinking of the problem of the double. Complications arose; Saul showed signs of imbalance and wanted to kill David. Jonathan helped him escape, and came to encourage him in exile by saying that David himself would

1. Of course the struggles of the biblical figures occurred on a much smaller scale. The majestic narratives should not (any more than should Homer's in another context) make us lose sight of the fact that these are just bitter feuds among tiny Bedouin tribes.

rule over Israel, while he would be David's devoted second.
Then during the chaotic warfare among the Hebrews, Philistines,
Transjordanians, etc., a bloody episode decimated the Hebrews
and caused the death of Saul and his three sons, including
Jonathan.

When David learned this, he showed intense grief. Here are
the last verses of his great funeral lament:

> O Jonathan, in your death I am stricken,
> I am desolate for you, Jonathan my brother.
> Very dear to me you were,
> your love to me more wonderful
> than the love of a woman.
>
> How did the heroes fall
> and the battle armor fail?

> (2 Sam. 1:26–27)

It is hard not to see that between these two young men there
was genuine feeling, which must have been homosexual since it
was between two men. Yet at no point in the narrative do we
find anything to suggest erotic passion or sexual relations. It is
not impossible, of course, but it is not stated. David compares
the love of Jonathan to the love of a woman, without exactly
seeming to disdain the latter. Subsequent events prove it: he
sees the wife of one of his officers standing on a terrace and is
captivated; he sends the officer to be killed in battle, a ruse to
get his widow. Was David homosexual "at heart," and heterosexual in terms of physical desire? I hardly need to say it would
be foolish to answer that question in view of the very slim
evidence we have.

When we turn to the Song of Songs, however, the contrast is
striking. Few texts in all of literature celebrate heterosexual love
with such poetry and erotic intensity. The book is generally

thought to be a collection of wedding songs. It glorifies the couple in love—through their violence, their sexuality, their world-excluding monogamy. Now this is a major text in the biblical tradition. The Song of Songs deals with the theme introduced by Hosea, considered in detail by Ezekiel, and taken up again much later by St. Paul: the love of the couple remains the best allegory for expressing the mysterious—even tragic—love between God and humanity.

People sometimes turn to the Bible for support when they want to glorify homosexuality (David and Jonathan), or to condemn it (Sodom). But I believe that doing either skirts the question entirely. There is no reason to project onto the Hebrew tradition moral or philosophical ideas which come from other places and much later times.

The World of Prison

Before getting to some remarks about the place of homosexuality in Western society today, I want to examine one popular belief. Does prison life induce homosexual tendencies?

This is no trivial question. If the answer is yes, we can conclude that sexual tendencies somehow reflect the culture or place where a person happens to be. In that case, homosexuality is just as "normal" as heterosexuality. This line of reasoning has, at times, been maintained. At the same time, if the answer is no, the situation is not so simple.

A psychoanalyst friend and I made a systematic study of the problem, since we had been asked to come up with a report. We conducted a series of interviews in various French prisons; we spoke with members of the staff, but most of all with the prisoners themselves. These were people being held awaiting trial, or short-term prisoners. We did not visit the penitentiaries, where prisoners were serving long or even life sentences, so we have only secondhand information in this area.

Contrary to popular belief, our data showed that a short period of imprisonment considerably reduces the sex drive. This seems to be true even in cases of sex offenders. It happens quite often that a man who is arrested repeatedly for hanging around the public toilets is at peace only during his spells in jail—as if there he were protected from something. Several prisoners freely gave me their own explanations. In jail the many pressures of the outside world are put aside. Meanwhile more immediate worries come to the fore: the progress of the case, the length of imprisonment, the chances of pardon or parole, concern for the future, cares about those who have been left outside, countless schemes to dodge the rules and make prison life more tolerable. These young men (average age: twenty-five) were married or going with women in normal life; they were surprised to find that their sexual activity seemed to limit itself of its own accord to occasional masturbation. Of course their reactions varied to some degree; personalities are always unique, and nonsexual offenses can reflect underlying sexual problems.

Among juvenille offenders some sex play may occur; but this is like what goes on among adolescents in a single-sex boarding school. It is not really a matter of homosexuality.

The proportion of true homosexuals does not seem to be any greater in jail than outside. In fact these people may be poorly accepted by the others, depending on the style of their homosexuality. As I understand it, the flirting gigolo types are poorly accepted in a cell with others. They may even have to be moved from cell to cell for their own protection.

To summarize the results of our investigation: "Do prisons make people homosexual?" The answer from those who had experienced prison life is unanimous—"Never! The ones who show signs of it were homosexual already." The study my psycho-analyst friend conducted independently was in total agree-ment.

Twenty or twenty-five years ago there was another field of observation: the memories of World War II prison camps were still fresh. It was just about this time that I began to study the question of homosexuality systematically, and I gathered a good deal of testimony. The data were especially interesting—pardon the expression—because these prisoners were taken by chance during a national disaster; they were not delinquents who could be assumed to have certain psychological problems already.

My overall impression is the same: homosexual practices were rare, and captivity, even of four years and more, did not make homosexuals out of men who were not so before. At times it brought out homosexuality which had been unrecognized or repressed; we will come back to this point. But for the most part the sex drive was muted, just as in civilian jails and for analogous reasons: the break with normal life, the burning emo-tional preoccupation with the conditions themselves, the defeat, and the hope of liberation.

Of course there were exceptions. Around 1950 I had several meetings with a forty-year-old man who wanted to talk about his problems. He had been married since before the war, and was the father of two. Yet he quite often had passing affairs with other men. He told me that when he had made love during the day "with a good-looking young cop," he could make love that night with his wife in a way that they both found more enjoyable. (She seemed to suspect nothing.) Then he talked about his captivity.

He was a reserve officer, and found himself in a prison camp along with a "magnificent" sergeant of twenty-five. The sergeant was already engaged to a young woman. Mutually attracted, the men became close friends who confided in each other. Soon the officer seduced the younger man, without much difficulty, it seems, and they formed an emotional and erotic homosexual relationship. "This boy was very much in love," added my visitor. "He gave himself to me in bed like a girl." I still remember that line.

Because of his health and age, the officer was freed before his friend, and returned to France. He looked up the charming fiancée, who was pining away for her captive sergeant. For love of him these two had sexual relations, each wishing the absent lover shared the bed. Then came 1945 and the liberation. The sergeant came home to his fiancée, and they were married. The officer remained their friend, but all homosexual relations stopped quite naturally.

Some years after our conversations, I learned by chance that this man had committed suicide by throwing himself under a train. It was during a period of depression that must have been bound up with his problem in some way.

This kind of story is most unusual, but it suggests that latent homosexuality can be touched off by special circumstances. Its appearance can be temporary, but it can also be permanent. There were several cases of married men who returned from captivity, left their wives, and went off with their lovers. Most often this led to a series of transient affairs.

In a very general way, I believe that our sexual orientation is fixed by age sixteen or seventeen. That means if the other has truly been reached, there is no going backwards. There is some evidence for this contention. I recall a messy scandal I became interested in because one of my clients was involved. About twenty boys, fourteen to seventeen years old, had been brought together by several adult pederasts on some cultural pretext. The boys had let themselves be "used," but as far as I know, not one of them became homosexual in the long run.

Yet latent—I would rather say unrecognized or repressed—homosexuality can, under certain conditions, break through a heterosexual camouflage. Again, there is no universal pattern or explanation; we are dealing with the stories of unique individuals. A short time in prison is clearly regressive in terms of autonomy, responsibility, monotony, and unisexual living. Perhaps in certain people that experience alone can reveal homosexuality they have until then rejected. But I believe this is rare —much rarer than is often claimed.

On the other hand, what occurs very often is a temporary regression in whatever sexual orientation exists. I am thinking of a twenty-eight-year-old man who has been delinquent since the age of sixteen or seventeen and periodically spends a few months in jail. The last time he was sentenced to two years. Whenever he is a prisoner he reverts to a sort of preadolescent calm. And his morale is excellent—this is the expression he uses when he writes to me.

Long-term imprisonment does seem to pose different problems, but since I didn't study it myself, I have to rely on the opinions of prison staff members; these data are highly inconsistent. It seems that during long imprisonment there is a tendency for homosexual pairs of a particular kind to be formed: an older man who is dominant and rather sadistic, and a younger one who is submissive and something of a slave. The atmosphere is charged with jealousy; murders can happen.

It would be foolish and dogmatic to draw any firm conclusions on this question of long imprisonment. After all, the real criminals—pimps, pushers, killers, and thieves—tend to be deeply disturbed in their whole emotional makeup. You do not just decide to become a criminal. I have seen that among these people the homosexual psychoaffective (but not necessarily erotic) pattern is very common, along with "dominant-dominated" relationships.

Our Western Culture

What is Westurn culture, anyway? When people talk about it they often append the term *Judeo-Christian*, which only adds to the confusion. It implies a pseudo-unity reminiscent of the Holy Roman Empire.

There are actually many Western cultures, and they are not, for the most part, based on the gospel. "What's true on this side of the Pyrenees is false on the other side." Even within the same country a common language and educational system do not erase cultural differences which predate the modern political entity and may be rooted in the distant past. In France, for instance, we might contrast the Basques with the Alsatians. It is no surprise that there are wide variations in the ways people respond to homosexuality. In the Basque country, which I know well, homosexuality seems to be quite rare; when it does occur, it is handled through a sort of tacit acceptance. So and so is still a boy at forty? People don't get upset; they accord him his place in society. For his part, he makes sure any affairs he has are conducted outside his own community, in a neighboring village perhaps. In other cultures, though, homosexuality is rejected with horror, and the person almost forced to leave town. In still others it is treated with an amused and condescending indulgence. Reality is highly diverse. Then, too, public opinion is inconsistent, depending as much on the personality of the party in question as on what he or she has presumably done. It would be absurd to imagine that we are dealing with anything as simple as "society versus the homosexuals."

Western culture has many traditions: Greco-Roman, Celtic, Germanic, Anglo-Saxon, Slavic, etc. Then again, we should really put all these adjectives in the plural. Homosexuality is surely not seen in the same way in Spain as in the Netherlands, in Italy as in Scotland. In fact there must be real differences between

Andalusia and Catalonia, or between Bavaria and East Prussia. What is the place of homosexuality in the various socialist societies of Eastern Europe? In each tradition, various underlying streams of thought mix—or clash: magic, Greek myth, dualism, Jansenism, eroticism, Puritanism, etc. Reality is an incredible hodge-podge; it is very different from that abstraction of "society versus the homosexuals" created by certain sociological mythmakers.

Let's try to understand how a person with homosexual tendencies actually relates to the surrounding human environment. This question, too, is more complex than it sounds. There are family relationships; there are neighbors, shopkeepers, casual acquaintances; there are colleagues at work; there are personal friendships. Each person clearly works out a unique pattern of interaction.

Twenty-year-old Pierre stands out in a crowd. His homosexual problem is obvious from his dress, his walk, his gestures, and his voice. People would describe him as effeminate, but he is really like a seductive little boy. When he left home there was no crisis; he just wanted to live his own life. He has no problems at all professionally, since everyone knows he is homosexual, and he knows that they know. It doesn't bother people at the office, and it doesn't bother him. If he goes to see a therapist it is because he has a phobia about his nose. He considers it ugly (though his features are really quite handsome); it makes him shy and keeps him from meeting the man of his dreams (who by definition, of course, does not exist). Yet he does not in any way feel rejected by "society" at large.

Robert is twenty-two. He is a bit clumsy, but his looks and mannerisms are completely normal. At the same time he finds it very hard to cope with his homosexuality in his everyday relations. There are huge problems with his family. Although he has a good position and is highly regarded professionally, he is terribly afraid his coworkers will find out he is homosexual and reject him. In spite of solid evidence to the contrary, he cannot free himself from this anxiety. At times of depression his delusions almost drive him mad. All this is clearly a function of his total affective development; his sexual tendencies are just one sign of a much deeper problem.

Michel, at twenty-five, sees his human environment in still another way. He is a rebel, and considering his background I must say he has reason to be. A poor and narrow-minded family; an unstable father; a "religious vocation" chosen by his mother; seminary life from age fourteen (!) in a small, quite neurotic religious community; sexual relations from this age on at the demand of a highly disturbed priest. It's all there. Michel is in revolt against "society." Other people notice nothing wrong with him except that he is a bit melancholy and abstracted. None of his friends or colleagues suspect that his tendencies are exclusively homosexual. "He just isn't the type," they say. Michel's revolt is quite specific: he does not accuse "society" of rejecting him because he is homosexual; he accuses it of cutting him off from the heterosexuality he wants but cannot attain. In fact, psychologically, this is the source of his problems. If Michel could channel his revolt in a positive way he might possibly be able to grow into heterosexual life. But can psychotherapy ever release all that unconscious anxiety and false, neurotic guilt?

Pierre, Robert, Michel. . . . These fictitious names correspond to real people I have known. But to avoid getting bogged down in too many clinical cases, I will sketch a composite portrait: certain men and women are explicitly homosexual in spite of their physical appearance and dress. Let's say their family lives are satisfactory, mainly because the other members allow them enough room for independence. In a similar way, the professional world may pose no major problems; they keep their work distinct from private life. This private life is varied and changeable: there are times of solitude, transient affairs, attempts to live with someone. But otherwise they follow an everyday routine in an average neighborhood. Their true friends are diverse, and a trusted heterosexual couple may be aware of their problem. Since they neither hide nor flaunt their tendencies, some of their acquaintances know of them and some do not. Those who don't know sometimes wonder why they stay single, yet their lifestyle doesn't encourage people to meddle. They have certain problems, yes. But they don't in any sense feel rejected by society because they are homosexual.

People often talk about segregation or sexual racism. This is no imaginary problem. We must deplore these attitudes and work to change them, since people with homosexual problems are as worthy of respect as the others. Yet segregation is a two-way street; we are dealing with a relationship, not a unilateral phenomenon. Of course this is not limited to the question of homosexuality. Some people, consciously or not, provoke segregation. They have a chip on their shoulders, or they assume from the start that people will reject them. The others have to be very alert to their own unconscious, or they will be trapped into playing the game and assuming an "anti" position.[2]

Here, too, current language can be revealing. People say, for example, "*We* Parisians" or "*We* scientists," or "*We* Catholics"— or even "*We* homosexuals." Right from the start, before giving anyone a chance, the speaker takes the stance of an opponent. There is usually a hint of superiority or militancy. We would like to reply, "Well, *we* Genevans, writers, Protestants . . . or heterosexuals. . . ."

---

2. If one manages to avoid playing the game, the provocateur may even be frustrated and angry. That happened to me with an anticlerical student from Quebec; he was taken aback not to find in me the clerical caricature he needed—legitimately—to oppose.

On the other hand, I have often heard people say something like: "When you are homosexual, you know, life has its bad moments." Now this is not segregative; the speaker is not looking for a fight, but simply trying to communicate. If segregation does occur, it will be the fault of the other party.

But what about the reactions of these other parties, the ones who have achieved some sort of heterosexuality? To a degree they are culturally conditioned. For instance, the prescientific idea of "nature" still pervades our society and affects people's moral judgments of homosexuality. Sexual stereotypes may also be involved. Thus people talk much more about male than about female homosexuality, and women tend to respond differently from men; they may be more "shocked" or more sympathetic.

Yet people are often inconsistent. In a private conversation or on a committee certain people will be very understanding; then in public they may revert to a sort of "moralistic" rigidity. We are never quite the same in private and in public.

Finally there is a deeper factor, which is rooted in the individual personality. Let's listen in on a discussion of homosexuality among people who are not directly concerned with the problem. Indirectly, of course, we are all involved in one way or another. There seem to be at least three types of response.

First of all there is a forty-year-old man who has done very well in his own life. He is happily married and a good father. The question interests him because he has several homosexual friends whom he respects and sympathizes with. He is a film producer, and enjoys his work. He would like to serve as a mediator, telling the public about the problem of homosexuality, and telling the homosexuals that they don't have to feel rejected. He can discuss his ideas calmly, even in the face of irate opposition. What bothers him most is that the homosexuals he knows are often isolated and unhappy. He can understand how they

feel; as a child he suffered from loneliness himself, but was able
to resolve it through his successful marriage. I must admit this
type of reaction is rare.

Others show a more casual interest in homosexuality. They feel
the question doesn't directly concern them. They know a number
of homosexuals through their work or through friends, and get
along with them the same as with anyone else. If somebody or
other is homosexual, so what? It is not their business and it
doesn't bother them at all. These people strike us as rather well-
balanced. They tend to have comfortable heterosexual lives and
an easy self-confidence. They can accept others as they are, without being upset by the odd or unconventional. Although people
might not think so, this type of reaction is quite common.

But there are always some who react violently. Of course their
indignation is based on "morality," or the "natural order of
things," or the "Law of God." If they should be talking with
people of the other two types they can come up with the most
outrageous statements: "Those people are sick! We should do
something about them; lock them up; castrate them; kill them!
It's revolting! They're dirty." Faced with such reactions, as I
quite often happen to be, my analyst's ears prick up. Why do they
care so much about the question of homosexuality? Isn't it a way
of protecting their own delicate sexual balance, or even a des-
perate denial of their own problem? Two or three of these moralists attacked me as vehemently as the writer of the article cited
in the Prologue. Yet I knew for a fact that these celibates, religious or not, were inordinately interested in young boys. On
several occasions they had barely avoided scandal because of
their social position. I could never make sense of their behavior:
where was the militant moralism when they were around more
or less cooperative adolescents? It is tempting to call it hypocrisy, but I actually think this incoherence was beyond their conscious control.

Another common phenomenon is equally hard to explain. As soon as a politician, or writer, or artist has made it to the top, the rumors start to circulate. "It seems he's . . . They say . . . You mean you don't know?" The innuendos do not refer to extra-marital affairs; if Mr. X or Mrs. Z takes a mistress or a lover, it doesn't merit such criticism in the gossip circles. No; these insinuations refer specifically to homosexuality, or to "unnatural acts"—generally with a hint of masochism. Several times I have tried to convince people that their suspicions were false; I knew personally that the subject of discussion might have some problems, but they were not of this variety. It was no use; people wanted to believe it. Perhaps it is a strange form of revenge. If a man gets too prominent he must have "something special," something both different and reprehensible. Success becomes a sort of anomaly, and enjoying it becomes hollow and scandalous. People seem to find this explanation reassuring, as if on an unconscious level they conclude: "Maybe I'm not famous, but *I'm* normal." As if you had to be neurotic to have talent or genius! But then again, so many neurotics—and homosexuals—have neither talent nor genius, while plenty of people who have aren't pathologically neurotic. This unfortunate cultural syndrome is related to what is called sexual racism.

One more cliché refers to homosexual social life, which is supposed to revolve around certain specialized "gay bars." Among the many people I have counseled, only a few talked of these places. On the other hand, they have mentioned a rather wide range of social groups. No doubt the variety, in fact, is considerably greater than I can realize from my vantage point.

First of all, there are many informal circles of friends. One of my clients, who belonged to such a group, asked me to come along to a few of their gatherings. The circle included seven or eight men of twenty-five to thirty-five. They had gotten to know each other in various ways, sometimes through the bars, and they met at members' homes once or twice a month. All of them were homosexual, but otherwise there was no simple common denominator, even social class. Yet as I understood it they did not get together mainly to talk about their problems or their latest affairs. They liked to talk about anything and everything—in an atmosphere of tacit mutual acceptance free of the subtle constraints of their everyday relationships. They knew something about my work, so they asked me to join them to discuss openly a question they considered very important: what their sexual problems meant in the light of their various religious conceptions. In the course of those few evenings of conversation I found I learned a lot myself.

In short this was a group of friends who preferred to meet among themselves rather than make the rounds of the nightclubs. It was something of an "in-group," but the segregative aspect was minor and certainly understandable. Each of these people had an entirely normal social life in addition to the circle.

The clubs are another gathering place for homosexuals. My visitors have told me a great deal about Arcadie, the best-known of such clubs in Paris. Here the segregative element seems much stronger, and the "regulars" may even refer to someone or other as a "convert." What goes on is rather complex. People do meet there who wind up having affairs. Yet this is not the focus of the club, and the atmosphere, so far as I know, is totally unlike that of the "gay bars." People go there to feel less alone, to be able to show their true selves. The club may really help them, for there is a functioning system of mutual aid: to find work, meet new people, share information—including legal advice if necessary, since the club's membership includes several lawyers.

A large club like Arcadie is obviously not selective in the way that groups of friends can be. This involves some risk in the presence of certain severe neurotics, pimps, etc. There is also the risk of segregation in creating a closed circle implicitly based on

opposition to "the others." A few of my visitors felt this strongly
enough to stop attending the club. Others, though, put up with
it as just one aspect of an organization whose focus was clearly
benevolent and fraternal.

There is a whole range of literary or artistic circles which function very differently from the clubs. Many of these circles seem
to follow a common pattern. First of all there are some central
figures—cultivated middle-aged men of means, often with ca-
reers in the arts; they tend to be rather flamboyantly homosexual.
They surround themselves with a shifting group of young people,
including a few women, all of whom are homosexual or ambivalent to some degree. Young men are chosen for aesthetic reasons;
they are like gigolos in style, and are usually going with someone
or other, for a while. There may also be a few boys who are not
homosexual at all but are brought into the circle by members who
find them physically attractive. It is through one of these boys
that I learned about a circle in which I was also counseling one
of the regulars. There is a good deal of snobbery, jealousy, and
selfishness; the affairs can be sordid. Yet on rare occasions true
and lasting friendships are established, most of the time without
sexual relations. The major element in these circles, however,
seems to be autosegregation.

We need only observe what happens on the patio or in the
lounge of some café on Saint-Germain-des-Prés to see that the
members of such circles like to go there. But in these cafés
the scene is more diverse, often more distressing. There are
the magnetic ones—rich gentlemen of the literary, filmmaking or
theatrical worlds—with their admirers, the social climbers, the
flops, and the gigolos. At a nearby table two of these middle-
aged men are talking: "You know little Claude? Really, he has
fantastic hips!" Perhaps they are discussing Claude and not just
his hips, but this is not usually the case. All this goes on in a
crowded square crossed by every segment of humanity. Furtive,

solitary passers-by are accosted by gigolos who are looking for homosexuals. They are often bisexual themselves, but sometimes their own tendencies are completely heterosexual. I have talked with some of these boys. They are lost: tragic childhoods, no family ties, no marketable skills, emotional isolation. Sometimes in their passing encounters they meet a man who doesn't stop with paying their price, but who helps them get out of this life, or at least does not treat them like merchandise. But often, seeing them walk the streets, I wonder sadly what can become of them. And I feel a mounting rage toward those rich gentlemen with their flatterers and their monstrous self-centeredness.

Now we still have to talk about the nightclubs. I mean the specialized places, the "gay bars" which cater almost exclusively to homosexuals. I'm in a very poor position to talk about them, since I have always felt a mixture of surprise and aversion toward such establishments, whether their clientele is homosexual or otherwise. Even as a student I never liked to shut myself up in a dark, crowded hole—where the atmosphere was filled with smoke and with music that was either bland or deafening; where a man could find not-too-bright girls; and where everyone had fun more or less desperately. Several times I have gone along with friends to some men's lounge, but I can never stand it for long. In every sense of the word, I need air.

What puzzles me most is how men can bring themselves to spend hours in such places. Quite a few homosexuals I have known feel the same way. Perhaps there is the hope of an encounter and a passing affair. Yet there is also something else, as my visitors describe it: the pleasure of being there, among men, talking about anything and everything, in the dark, enclosed environment cut off from the outside world. "Protected," we would be inclined to say. The segregative element is central. On an analytic level it is hard to avoid the image of a vast womb where the wounded or distressed instinctively retreat. As for me,

I left each time with a sense of sadness that was slow to dissipate.

The observations that I have made have led me to believe that in Western culture today, people with homosexual tendencies interact with the rest of the population in a great variety of ways. The scene cannot be reduced to any linear abstraction such as "society accepts heterosexuals," or "society rejects homosexuals." After all, what is "society?" Is it the complex diversified reality surrounding one legal system, or a figment of the speaker's imagination?

Vision is selective. One of my visitors spoke of his own experiences and observations in a way that brings this home. He haunted the Boulevard de Sebastopol, where there were several public toilets dedicated to the shades of the Emperor Vespasian. There at the end of the day he was sure to find all the partners he wanted, since, as he explained, all the men who walked down this boulevard at this time did so for this reason. That seemed exaggerated to me, in spite of my desire to believe him. Actually the explanation was quite simple: he only saw those men who entered the toilets in question and who went for this purpose. He did not see the crowd of men who rushed toward the nearest Metro station, perhaps without even noticing there were any urinals on the way, or those who entered the toilets with the simple need they were officially designed to serve.

This phenomenon of selectivity is absolutely universal, a function of each person's own psychoaffective structure. There is no reason to suppose that someone who is homosexual will escape it.

We often hear it said that society is repressive toward homosexuals. In the case of French legislation, this is simply not true, although it was true in the case of British law until very recently.[3] French law does not consider homosexuality *as such* a

3. In the United States, however, certain homosexual relations are still considered criminal in thirty-six states. On March 29, 1976, the U.S. Su-

crime. Private homosexual relations are not prohibited and are no concern of the authorities. Only when public order is threatened by sexual activity—of any variety—does the law step in: perversion of minors, public offense to decency. Certain points of application are still not beyond criticism, of course. If the police happen to surprise a man and a woman, or two men or two women, making love in a car parked on a deserted lane in the woods, the law applies (unless the officers have some sense, which is more common than folklore suggests): it is a public place. On the other hand, if a couple frolic naked in a room with an open window overlooking a narrow street, letting neighbors across the way enjoy the scene, nothing can be done: it is private property.

Decency itself is a vague and shifting notion. There has recently been a campaign against women going topless on the beach. People talk indignantly about the offense to decency, to public morality. For myself I suspect it is more often an offense to aesthetics. Why not denounce it on that score?

But let's get back to the point: French law does not repress private homosexual activity any more than private heterosexual activity. We could even say that homosexuality is less restricted: it cannot be cited in adultery cases.

---

preme Court ruled that the "right to privacy" does not protect homosexual relationships. The court affirmed the decision of a federal district court upholding a Virginia law that makes anal or oral homosexual intercourse a crime punishable by up to five years in prison and a $1000 fine. The Supreme Court ruling means that states may prohibit even homosexual acts performed in private by consenting adults.

In Canada, on the other hand, there have been no special restrictions on homosexuality since the 1969 omnibus amendment to the Criminal Code. Introduced by then-Minister of Justice Pierre Trudeau with the remark, "Government has no business in the bedroom," the amendment places homosexual activity in private between consenting adults outside the domain of criminal law—Tr.

Where problems do appear is in the mentality of those who enforce the law, the police and magistrates. Here we return to the basic question: how do these men and women relate to their own sexuality? On the basis of my clients' experiences I can readily conclude that some police officers are balanced while others are perverse; some judges are level-headed while others show signs of disturbance. This is no surprise. But it would be quite unfair to claim that the police and courts in general are obsessed with the idea of suppressing homosexuality. We need only observe the tact shown by the police when partners are clearly being recruited in certain locales. If there is an occasional raid, quite often it is for some other reason: drug traffic, or a search for specific people in connection with activities that *are* against the law.

For several years I knew two men who made the rounds of the public toilets. One took hardly any precautions, and went out whenever and wherever he pleased; he was never caught. The other was a bit anxious and seldom got up the nerve to go; he was apprehended three times in two years by the vice squad. Why? This is obviously more than just chance. Both men were respectable on other scores, but something in their contrasting personalities made one of them more vulnerable. Two of the three times, according to the second man himself, he dealt with officers who acted properly, a police chief who tried to understand, a magistrate who felt obliged to enforce the law, but who did it minimally, almost as a gesture. Sex offenders are well aware that with Judge X they will get off without any great fuss, while Judge Y will "throw the book at them."

The model of the repressive society is false to real experience because it is a model. Admittedly there is a general tendency, especially in some circles, to scorn homosexuals. However, I don't believe at all that this is universally dominant. Paradoxi-

cally, this prejudice is no less common among those who denounce "middle-class values." People on the "Left" can be just as
puritanical and rigid as people on the "Right."

A number of homosexual activists even refer to themselves as
revolutionaries.[4] I have met a few of them. Their main theme is
that they are persecuted by "society" because they are homosexuals; and now, instead of being persecuted, they want to
persecute others. They cannot discuss any of the subtler aspects
of the question. I know that if some of these revolutionaries
skim through this book and read the present passage I will be
vilified. Yet these people fail to see the magnitude of some
homosexual problems, or their diversity. For them everything
revolves around one central idea; and if we do not agree with
them immediately on every score we must be "against them,"
persecuting them. The attitude can be found in other than sexual
areas: Léon Bloy reacted this way with regard to his campaign
to canonize Christopher Columbus. These individuals often feel
they have some sort of mission as righters of wrongs. They lead
movements and demonstrations; people who are weak and easily
led get fascinated with them for a while. These revolutionaries
are proof of a strange logic which is rigorous yet incoherent by
the very fact of its rigor. I'm reminded of the words of Chesterton: "the fools have lost everything but their reason." No ex-
change of ideas is possible.

Chesterton's description also applies to people who adopt this
rigid stance on other issues, such as on the infallibility of the
Pope, and it explains a familiar term that is often misunderstood:
the *paranoid syndrome*. When this attitude is aggressively dis-

---

4. That there is need for a revolution in our times seems clear. For that
matter, shouldn't life be a permanent revolution against the prison of structures which always tend to become fixed? But to make homosexual tendencies the motive force leading to these changes, that is something else.

played it turns other people off, and makes them hostile. The reaction is understandable, since on an unconscious level paranoia is an aggressive defense against panic. Such people *are* in fact terribly threatening.

This peculiar affective structure is not necessarily accompanied by pathological raving. I have known people who were both brilliant and paranoid: moralists, Maoists, Thomists, militarists, dadaists, chauvinists, pacifists, etc. Homosexual tendencies can be the basis of this syndrome, though the link between paranoia and homosexuality is not so close or consistent as Freud once thought.

Since 1968 homosexual men—and women—have often become leaders of movements, fronts, organizations, and demonstrations. The results have been truly ambiguous. At last people can talk about homosexuality openly and less heatedly, but there are drawbacks in the form of confusion and emotional backlash. The confusion is apparent in the array of "types" one can observe at demonstrations: paranoid leaders; a majority, no doubt, whose motives are serious and rational; exhibitionists; hangers-on; and clowns. One of the movement's most confusing and annoying themes is what I'd like to call *sociologism*; the "ism" refers to a closed system of thought which ignores the complexity of reality. We catch a whiff here of the badly digested theories of Wilhelm Reich.

People who work in the physical sciences and study measurable data are not in much danger of jumping to philosophical conclusions (though a few biologists have come close). But in talking about the human personality we run a great risk of oversimplifying the facts on the basis of theoretical "isms."

Psychoanalysis reveals the very facts which all cultural, philosophical, and "religious" movements tend to mask: the dizzying ambivalence of human relationships which are themselves complex and hard to pin down. This vertigo is rooted in the presence of sexual duality and death. Each and every one of us is threatened to some degree by the intrusion of the other who is different. Such feelings are relentlessly unveiled in the course of real psychoanalysis. But the facts are hard to accept, because they show the insufficiency of reason and the total impotence of human beings to resolve, once and for all, their constitutional anxiety.

The Myth of "Society"

One of our current defenses against this vertigo is *sociologism*,[5] a hasty generalization from sociological data. It is really an unconscious way of evading the dilemma of human relations. There must always be a tension between individualism, which denies the importance of the group, and collectivism, which ignores the matter of individuals. But it is mind-boggling to consider the demands and mechanisms of social groups at the same time as the uniqueness of the people involved. The synthesis, the final solution to this dialectic, is totally beyond us. So we find a scapegoat in "society," a mythic entity conceived as repressive.

Mythic entity: real society is a group of human beings who muddle through life on traditional data of mental symbolization and practical organization. A given society is the result of a long, slow process, of people's efforts first to survive, then to make the best possible life for themselves. How did human beings first emerge from a state of nature? We cannot know scientifically. But nowhere does there exist, in some sort of neo-Platonic heaven, a "Society in itself," an ambivalent goddess somehow predating or transcending history.

5. There is also *psychoanalysm* or *psychologism*, of course. We will get to them in the next chapter.

Repressive reality: but of course. If people all did exactly what they pleased, nobody would survive. This basic point is often misrepresented by sociologism. It is amazing how often freedom of expression means claiming the whole arena for self-expression, and preventing others from expressing themselves. In the name of freedom of expression, activists in Gay Liberation or Women's Liberation disrupt meetings where people are actually trying to understand sexuality and to free themselves of taboos. There is a strange incoherence.

People accuse "society" of being repressive and imposing restrictions. Actually two quite different issues are involved. With regard to homosexuality, people may be talking about the moralistic prejudices which should, in fact, be criticized. But they may gloss over entirely the basic need for restrictions during the first years of life if the child's affective personality is to grow freely. Certain Freudian ethnologists—they can hardly be called analysts—ignore this fact completely. In all personality development, it is the primal restrictions which first give rise to desire and make further growth possible. A child cast from birth into a world without any restrictions would not survive more than a couple of days. Clinical evidence shows that it is the lack of structure—or its distortion—that later produces the great neurotics, obsessives, and schizophrenics.

It is the confrontation with the prohibited desire for incest that opens the way to all other possibilities. In our culture the incest taboo appears in the guise of the Oedipal conflict. Without trying to reduce the whole issue to psychogenesis, I want to suggest that it is often the inconsistency of the Oedipal conflict which keeps some persons from reaching heterosexuality. We can say schematically that when the mother is not forbidden as an object of possession, it is the woman who will be forbidden as the object of desire. This formula does not come from wild imagination; it is an attempt to make sense of clinical reality. When people talk of "repressive society" we can well ask what specter of their own sexuality lurks behind this mythic idea.

For a number of years such notions have found their way into the language of many clients. I sense, however, that the influence is superficial and that the speakers are not really taken in. A man in his twenties asks to see me. He arrives saying something like this: "I am a homosexual. Society rejects *us*. *They* won't let *us* live." Now this person knows who I am, and that I am neither a sociologist nor a politician. Then why does he come to see me? The very fact that he does, suggests that what he really wants is quite different from what he says. The militant, paranoid types do not ask to see me, except at times to denounce me as the incarnation of "repressive society," which is always rather funny. The people who do come are troubled and want help.

Men and women with homosexual tendencies must not be regarded as sinners or outcasts; we must work for a radical change in public opinion on this score. But such attitudes cannot change if certain people, by their own aggressive stance, provoke rejection and alienate even those with the best of intentions. I hope the majority of homosexual people will not let themselves be manipulated by such dubious leaders.

5. Human Lives and Morals

The Helping Relationship

It is a recent phenomenon: for twenty years or so, people faced with life problems have been turning to professionals for help. What was rare in the thirties has become a matter of course since Freudian insights have transformed psychology and influenced social service, medicine, and religion.

Fifty years ago, a frigid woman scarcely thought she had a problem. Over the course of time, however, the condition came to be considered unsatisfactory, so that now the woman—or the couple—"gets help." An impotent man "gets help" in the same way. Today we know that both these problems are usually the province of clinical psychology.

But in other days people consulted a doctor, if anyone. I recall a story my father, a surgeon and urologist, told me. Shortly before World War I he was visited by a couple who had been married about six months but had not yet managed to have sexual intercourse. It was a case of incredible ignorance, but quickly solved; my father added—without mentioning his name, of course—that the "product" of that consultation was one of my acquaintances.

Then again, people who were practicing Catholics often talked to a confessor. I am convinced that certain sensible, balanced, experienced confessors did an excellent job of psychotherapy even if they had never heard the word.

For the past thirty years the person consulted is more and more often a *psychologist* (a term which is highly ambiguous). Among people with homosexual tendencies, there seems to be just a small minority who do not feel it to be a life problem. Perhaps some work things out on their own, without recourse to anybody. I can only state from my own experience that many do feel the need to talk about it. They go to a counselor for help in dealing with their problems. This is not new, of course. Gide himself consulted a psychiatrist; at the turn of the century, it is not surprising that the response was advice: "Get married, that will take care of you." We know what happened in his case.

Thus I cannot stress too strongly one basic necessity: a psychologist must discard the concept and the word *treatment*. Fifteen or twenty years ago I could not have written that. Treatment inevitably suggests a very specific kind of relationship. Mr. Dupont has had a stomach ache for some time. He goes to a gastroenterologist, someone who may have "knowledge" about him that he himself lacks. He puts himself "in the hands of" a specialist. There are clinical examinations, Xrays, laboratory tests. The diagnosis is made: Mr. Dupont has an ulcer. The specialist then proposes "treatment" and gives "advice": rest, diet, maybe an operation. Thus there is something the doctor "does," while the sick person agrees to "undergo" treatment.

It is an entirely different matter when someone asks for help with the problem of homosexuality. We have already seen that the term *illness* is not applicable. As a comparison, let's suppose Mr. Durand is struggling with an awkward problem and is not having much success on his own. He goes "to talk with someone about it," someone, of course, who is experienced and a "good counselor." Now suppose this someone is a man who listens, knowing deep down that he has no secret solution, but who is

trying to understand piece by piece what Mr. Durand is telling
him. He will not say much at all. He will ask only brief, discreet
questions to give Mr. Durand the chance to clarify certain points
he may have glossed over. (Why, incidentally? But that's another
question.) After a few of these conversations Mr. Durand will
begin to work out his own solution. The person he went to see
is a good counselor precisely because he gives no "advice."[1] We
would not consider using the word treatment for this kind of
relationship.

This very danger of returning to the notion of treatment is implied by a certain style of psychology. Freud discovered the
unconscious, not by philosophical thought, but by a clinical
mode of access to the inner life of his patients. To pass on his
discoveries, he developed a theory of psychic organization, and
described the stages of the affective life. In this sense he is
analogous to Pasteur, who discovered microorganisms. Pasteur's
discoveries unsettled traditional ideas in philosophy on the subject of life and its generation; but most of all they brought
therapeutic advances: serums, vaccines, asepsis, and modern
surgery. Freud's discoveries, in the same way, unsettled traditional ideas in philosophy on the soul, on freedom, on morality,
and overturned the accepted therapeutic approach to neurosis and
psychosis. But there the comparison ends. This is the error of a
certain psychologism or psychoanalysm: Freudian insights are
misused as therapeutic weapons, another kind of treatment a
doctor can apply to a patient.

Let's imagine a male psychiatrist, or nonmedical "psycho-
something-or-other." He has *read* Freud and other writers in

1. I remember a woman who came to see me in a state of turmoil and
anxiety. For about an hour I listened to her, without saying anything but
"Ah?" "Oh, yes," "I understand." Then she rose to leave, not wanting to
take any more of my time. On the doorstep she added warmly, "Oh, thank
you for everything you told me!" No doubt she had never truly been able
to talk, and so to understand herself.

the field; he has "understood" the psychic organization and the stages of the affective life. When a young man consults him because he is having problems with homosexual tendencies, he listens a little, but mainly asks questions and offers explanations and advice.

"Ask questions" . . . But which ones? He asks questions on the basis of his own theories, because certain signs relate to what he has learned from the books. In the same way a physician will ask a patient he is examing: "Do you cough up a lot of mucus when you first get up in the morning?" Certain signs make him suspect the problem is chronic bronchitis, and he knows from the books that this is a basic symptom. In that case the question is legitimate. The "psycho-something-or-other," who has a "thorough knowledge of the Oedipus complex," will ask: "Are you very close to your mother?" without realizing in the slightest that he is asking this question primarily in terms of his own relationship to his own mother.

"Offer explanations" . . . This is always tempting. By giving explanations we first of all tell ourselves that we have understood, that we have covered the problem. We tell our clients this, too, and signal them that they have nothing more to say. The "psycho-something-or-other" will show a client how to apply to his "case" the formula of the Oedipal "mechanism." If the client ever tells him a dream, he will easily find in it proof of his explanation. We can find what we want to in dreams, especially other people's dreams. But we will obviously lose any chance of understanding what they mean, what they want to say. It is the "psycho-something-or-other" who is heard, not the person who asked for help.

"Offer advice" . . . This is a big temptation since even the visitor often requests it. We will say: "Do this . . ." or: "You should . . ." or: "If you do this, probably . . ." We thus literally dismiss our clients as autonomous people; we try to act in their place: "If I were you . . ." We want to induce them, out of some hunger for power, to behave as we think they should behave, to conform to our wishes. This is all unconscious, of course; at the end of chapter 1 I described a relationship I blundered into with a client, and how it made me aware of the whole process.

Unfortunately such an attitude is still very common. It is the source of the notorious advice to use prostitutes or marriage to cure homosexuality. Men and women have often—even today—come to consult me because their psychoanalysts urged them to go to the Pigalle or to take a lover. I reply: "If he really told you that he is not a psychoanalyst; or if he is, in fact, a psychoanalyst he told you nothing, in which case you and he have got to analyze why you thought he wanted such a thing."

All in all it is hard to find the right word for the true helping relationship. *Care* and *psychotherapy* are still inadequate, for they send us back to the idea of treatment. It is not a matter of taking care of people, but of helping them.

"Helping them"—to do what? First of all, remember that you can only help someone who, in one way or another, asks for it. This sounds like a cliché, but how many people try to aid someone who personally feels no need of help; what they can see of the other's problems is disturbing *them*! On several occasions I've received an agitated phone call from a mother who has just learned that her son is homosexual:

"Could you see him, and help him change?"

"Does he want to change?"

"That's just what worries me; he doesn't seem to."

"Well then?"

"But he's such an impressionable child, if you only knew!"

"How old is he?"

"Twenty-seven."

"Does he know you are calling me?"

"Oh, no. I didn't breathe a word to him! If you could just get him to meet you on some pretext."

"But Madam, your son is not a little boy anymore."

(A pause) "Yes, I know, but . . ."

"How about this: Why not tell your son you phoned me. Tell him I said that if he wants to see me I'm available and he is welcome to contact me directly."

"But you couldn't give me an appointment for him?"

"I never make appointments by proxy."

Sometimes the mother understood. Occasionally she asked to see me herself, to discuss her own problems in dealing with the situation. I would agree, adding that I would not in that case be able to work with her son, but that he could consult X, Y, or Z (I'd recommend several therapists) if he wished.

Sometimes the conversation ended right there. But quite often the son did make an appointment. It might be solely to please his mother, and to satisfy himself that I had nothing to tell him. Or it might be a chance for him to talk freely about his problem, because he saw me as truly distinct from his mother's desires.

In this helping relationship, what really matters is the autonomy of the person who comes to us. So the counselor needs a very clear understanding of his or her own desires. After all, the counselor has to want something in the relationship. And the wrong kind of desire can make it impossible to help people (see pp. 29-30). The desire to cure their patients is normal for physicians; yet this involves more than the simple desire that the patients get well. There is also the desire to come across—to their patients and to themselves—as good doctors, competent and effective. If they felt otherwise they would, in fact, be bad doctors. This pattern of desire is destructive in the case of a counselor working with homosexual clients.

The forty-year-old patient with bronchial pneumonia has a burning desire first of all not to die, and then to recover as soon as possible and return to normal life. On the other hand, it is not at all certain that a homosexual has any desire to change. By definition this person has no experience of anything else, and can't desire to return to a normal life that has been interrupted by illness. Often, though, there is an explicit desire for change: "I want to be like the others, like my friends—to love a woman and to have children." Yet the problem is that the counselor has no power to create the change in him. Still another problem is that the client's unconscious desire may not be the same as his explicit desire. A man may want to change much less than he believes in all sincerity.

This is easy enough to understand. He has no experience of growing personally through heterosexual attraction and fulfillment. Changing means first of all renouncing the experience he does know, and which, even if it causes him pain, still brings him some pleasure too. He must frustrate this satisfaction for a new one, which by definition does not really appeal to him at this point. Some individuals do arrive at heterosexuality via the route of psychotherapy (see chapter 1). But I believe they are a real minority.

Then what is the legitimate desire of the counselor, whose role is essentially different from that of the doctor? It cannot be the desire to influence the visitor to change—not without completely distorting the relationship. The desire to cure has no place here. I think, though, we can put it this way: the good counselor desires, by listening, to help people know themselves. Clients decipher their own stories, and analyze for themselves what happens in this special helping relationship; at the end, if possible, they find their skin fits better. Occasionally they may find themselves right on the threshold of heterosexuality—if so, well and good; it is one of many possibilities. The counselor's narcissistic satisfaction is still there, of course: we are glad to be good psychotherapists. The point is to know what we mean by that.

Something clearly takes place through this helping relationship. But whatever happens is unlike a conversation, a discussion, or a friendship. Here I must introduce technical terminology and speak of transference. It is a reciprocal process: something happens in the client, but something equally important happens in the counselor.

A recent experience will help me get this across better than a statement of theory. I say "experience," not "case." A person's "case" is fixed, like an object over there, or like an insect under observation. The psychotherapist—since we have no better word —is neither an observer nor an entomologist, but a participant in what takes place.

He was about twenty. I think he decided to consult me after hearing one of his professors mention my work. He was starting medical school—a magnificent, handsome-faced six-footer, a basketball champion. He had no problems with homosexuality, since he was strongly attracted to women, and to one in particular. But behind the calm, athletic appearance lurked a deep and abiding malaise over impotence, and not just in the sexual sense.

We agreed to begin meeting. Our sessions, one or two per week, went on for about three years. At first he projected onto me the mythic role of the "One Who Knows." Without realizing it, he made me a sort of transcendent being with the last word, the key to his problems. Then came the time when he saw what he was doing, and also that I was no such being. I obviously had to avoid playing this role, even in my own eyes; I had to accept knowing nothing.

Then he began to relive through me his hidden, archaic responses to his mother, his father, his brothers. I can't go into detail here about his dreams, free association, and overall itinerary—that would take volumes. But gradually he saw that his problem involved a truly homosexual anxiety in relation to his father. He had felt it in early childhood, but only realized it explicitly when he felt it again toward me. The implication was that he had not resolved this problem at the usual time. As the oldest boy, he felt himself the focus of desire of a father who was dissatisfied in his marital relationship (which was no doubt the case). The results were submission to this desire, rebellion to free himself, and guilt over this rebellion. He found himself trapped between his problem and the successive arrival of three brothers.

Gradually, first without realizing it, then more consciously, at last systematically, he found himself in relation to his past; whether real or imagined, it was the past as he had lived it. He plunged again into this emotionally very primitive time; then he freed himself and grew to see it as his own past, yet over with. The whole process was made possible through the relationship that he and I had voluntarily assumed.

The final months were a thrilling experience. I said almost nothing, but he could tell me what he had never before been able to say. All the while he clearly dissociated the spectral figure he was struggling with from my real self across from him. My chair was behind my desk, with its back to a blank wall between two windows. He began to locate the spectral figure behind the curtain of one of the windows. He would explain to me what he was saying to the presence and analyze his own development with remarkable insight. Toward the end, his problem was how to bring himself to leave me in such a way that this specter— which was neutralized and put in its place, but not at all destroyed —stayed "behind *the* curtain," not "behind *my* curtain." I can find no better way to express the deep meaning of his progress. He had really found his way out. At the end of the last session he groped a bit for words as he paused on the threshold; then, with a totally effortless smile, he said: "Well, then. Carry on!" This was his free, "potent" acknowledgement that each of us would continue his own journey. I had never, of course, given him any sign either of sympathy or of disapproval, but at that point I thought it good to put a hand on his shoulder, return his smile, and add: "You too, friend." I don't think I will see him again; I could even say I hope not. That would prove that each of us together achieved something.

Here I would like to stress one essential point. My countertransference was positive: I really liked him, and was glad to see him come for his sessions. Yet while realizing this, it was crucial that I attach no value to it for myself. That means that if one day he had decided not to come any more, it would be all the same to me, even in terms of my frustration as therapist. It was clear to me that if I desired even deep down that he become potent, I would have interfered with his growth. I would have plunged him back into his conflict, into the childish submission to adult desires. I had to beware of that, because I did like him and admired his intelligence. He was perhaps a future colleague, and I could very easily have desired to see him as a psychotherapist too—my disciple, to carry on my work.

Thinking about this experience at a distance of several months, I have come up with a schematic description; it may sound strange, even shocking, but I think it fits the facts. In all that was said, overtly and between the lines, we lived for about three years in a normal homosexual—or homosexed, if you prefer—relationship. This allowed him to emerge from a homosexual dialectic which, during childhood, had become badly entangled with the father figure, the image of the man in relation to woman.

From now on he must be able to love a woman, to make love with her, and to become a father himself.

Homosexual Tendencies and Marriage

People often ask, "Is it good for a homosexual man or woman to get married?"

Sometimes the homosexual parties ask the question on their own account as they seek counseling. Their families may be urging them to marry, or they may be wondering themselves: "Couldn't I be like everyone else?" "Couldn't marriage cure me?" A homosexual man may find that a woman has fallen in love with him; he hesitates because of his tendencies, though he may like her a great deal.

Sometimes the woman herself comes to ask the question. She is worried in spite of herself about a future she desires and dreads at the same time. Sometimes it is a counselor, lawyer, or confessor who has not studied the problem and who wants to clarify matters by consulting a "specialist."

Now here, too, it would be presumptuous to think we can come up with any definitive answer. After twenty years of experience I tend to reply cautiously, "In general it doesn't make things any better." Yet it is not quite so simple. I have on several occasions seen a good, enduring marriage between a man with strong homosexual tendencies (that is, ambivalent), and a woman who seemed to have no sexual problems.

I knew one man in this situation whose homosexuality remained beneath the surface. But it shaped his need to help young people socially or professionally. He didn't deceive himself about the source of this need, and could admit that he was strongly attracted emotionally and physically to certain boys. Fortunately he and his wife shared a truly rich marriage, and a warm relationship with their four children. This, in fact, was what freed him from being drawn into affairs which for him would have been disastrous. On his silver wedding anniversary he could point to a generally positive balance sheet.

I knew another man who was equally ambivalent, and who also achieved a rather stable marriage. But from time to time he continued to have his "weaknesses," as he put it, with one of the homosexuals he knew.

Sometimes, however, a young man has been so influenced by his cultural background that he hides his tendencies even from himself, or thinks they will go away. He is encouraged when he meets a woman who strongly attracts him and he marries her. For fifteen or twenty years there is no problem. He and his wife get along well, they have a good sex life, their children are born and grow up. Then at forty-five or fifty, with age and its inevitable complications, the tendency toward homosexuality revives—much as he continues to love his wife. My impression is that a couple's chances of success are really threatened in such cases. The marriages I have known where things still worked out for the best seem to be the exceptions.

Several kinds of marriages involving homosexuals can be described. The following sketches are based on clinical observation, but they are not, of course, exhaustive.

A homosexual boy may be pressured by his family into marrying a suitable young woman in order to conform to the unwritten rules of their social class. Of course the pressure is subtle: there may be talk of his allowance, or of his future position in the family business. This situation undoubtedly occurs less often today than fifty years ago, but I have known several examples.

The marriage is a great social event: a formal church wedding, a big reception in a luxury hotel. But the main character lives through all this like a march to the gallows. The bride does not suspect the problem the boy's family has passed on to her. "Alone at last," the scene explodes. Although he may really like her, the young husband is incapable of the slightest physical desire for the woman who is there, wanting him. Yet it may take several years for the "marriage" to become unbearable for one or the other of them; the wall of social convention is strong.

The wife puts up with her husband's more and more frequent nights out and his more and more palpable absence. Then one day she meets another man. This one is heterosexual, and the prospect of a real married life with him seems possible and desirable. Then comes the complicated issue of divorce. Once I had the genuine satisfaction of telling the young man's parents exactly what I thought of their attitude, which was nothing short of criminal. The families involved were "good Catholics." The scandal of divorce could not be tolerated unless it was accompanied by a Church annulment; only then would the young wife be able to remarry decently.

At the time, however (many years before Vatican II), the ecclesiastical courts showed a hermetic ignorance of psychological reality. They worked only according to legalistic criteria. An annulment was out of the question, even on the grounds of non-consummation: the bride had not been a virgin. In this case the young man's parents and their ecclesiastical accomplices share the responsibility for two wrecked lives.

A rather common situation is the neurotic couple who are drawn to each other spontaneously. A woman selectively falls in love with a man who is homosexual, or at least very ambivalent; on his part, he finds a certain satisfaction in this stunted emotional relationship. They get married. Quite often the wife knows beforehand the seriousness of her partner's homosexual problem. The situation may go on indefinitely, but it rarely does, since in psychological terms it is much more of a mother-child relationship than a true couple. That can not be endured for long except if it becomes a *modus vivendi*, letting them live together as good friends.

It is also no accident—even if she does not know it consciously—when a woman falls in love with a man who is sexually impotent with women. Here, too, can we call this a marriage in the full sense of the term? Until very recently when the religious—or canonical, which is quite different—question arose, the roadblocks were the same as in the previous case of homosexuality. It was nearly impossible to get an official annulment of such a "marriage," regardless of the psychological evidence. This could turn out to be a grave handicap for the wife if she developed a desire for a true marriage. On several occasions I have helped a young woman who found herself in this position to cross the social and pseudo-Christian taboos with a clear conscience.

The reverse situation can be seen as well. A man who seems, to himself and to others, entirely heterosexual selectively falls in love with a woman who is mannish and consciously homosexual. And the feeling is mutual. They establish a highly complex relationship, which can take the form of a marriage. With what specter does each of them, through the other, make love? Generally the relationship does not last, but if there are children, which is quite possible, they tend to be disturbed from the start.

In each of these sketches the same question comes to mind. Under these conditions, when one or the other of the parties is aware of the homosexual problem, why do they want marriage— a state which is oriented toward the other? Of course there is no simple answer; the motivation is unique to each individual.

But is a laissez-faire policy desirable on the part of a friend, doctor, lawyer, confessor, etc.? It seems to me that people always have the right to express an opinion, and any reservations they may have; not, however, to authorize or to prohibit. Then again, everything I have said is just my own view of a reality which cannot be pinned down. As for the marriage of homosexuals, I don't believe there is any absolute rule.

One point does, however, strike me as generally valid. If a man or woman who is homosexual is considering marriage, the question needs to be explored in depth and at leisure. I feel the person should be able to talk it over in the context of a helping relationship with a true psychological counselor: one who is neutral, trying not, even unconsciously, to exert pressure of any kind.

Changing a Mentality

If we accept the average of many statistical studies, we can assume that 7 percent of the male population is concerned with the problem of homosexuality. Out of a hundred men there should thus be about seven who have explicit homosexual tendencies, exclusive or otherwise. On Bastille Day, in the midst of revising this book, I thought of applying the statistic. The idea is not nearly so farfetched as it sounds.

Fifteen thousand men filed past hundreds of thousands of people who lined the streets between the Bastille and the République. If we consider only the population of young males who were marching, 1050 homosexuals—statistically speaking—must have passed by. Yet people did not distinguish them from the others. Suppose we estimate the crowd of both sexes who watched at 300,000; let's apply the statistic, assuming the figure of 7 percent also holds true for women. There were then some 21,000 homosexuals looking on. Yet again, with very rare exceptions, they were not noticed. The homosexuals really *are* just like the others.

I wonder how my neighbors in the crowd would have reacted if I had announced: "Say, do you know that of these 15,000 men passing before us, about 1050 are probably homosexuals." The idea would certainly have surprised them. I can imagine several responses:

Indignant: "What! You don't mean that! Never! This is the French Army!"

Amused: "Well, well, how strange. I never would have guessed it."

Interested: "You could tell just by watching them go by?"

Still more interested: "I was hoping there would be more. They were such good-looking boys, weren't they? Then, too, that uniform."

Speechless: a dark look.

But most often, I think, we would get a common-sense reaction: "So what? Why should I care?" I believe this would be the dominant one. At least, I hope so, since it indicates an intelligent apprehension of the situation: nothing to worry about, one way or the other. In statistical terms, I'm convinced that of the 93 percent of the population who are heterosexual, 50 or 60 percent are generally comfortable with their own sexuality.

Yet according to my many visitors, public opinion is still often a problem, and not in a purely subjective way. Most of the time they have the feeling that they must carefully conceal their sexual orientation so as not to be rejected. Some find it very hard to have to play a role. Although this is clearly a subjective reaction, it just as clearly has some objective basis. In any social circle, how would family, co-workers, and neighbors respond if they knew for certain that Mr. X or Miss Y was homosexual? I believe it is absolutely necessary to change the widespread, dominant mentality.

Two main ideas seem to underlie or influence this mentality. Most often people are not even aware of these assumptions, but at times they are expressed openly.

The first assumption is that homosexual tendencies are a *defect*: a grave handicap which devalues human potential for success. To push it a bit further, it would be something like mongolism or a major congenital deformity. Now this is false on all scores. It is not a congenital situation; and if we look around us it is plain that the lives of a good many homosexuals are just as successful as those of heterosexuals. Of course success in its usual sense (personal qualities; social, humanitarian, scientific, and other achievements) is not a function of either homo- or heterosexuality. I believe we can even say that for certain individuals who are gifted in other ways, their homosexual tendencies—though painful—serve as a stimulus; such people compensate for their lack of emotional satisfaction through activities which are valued socially. The fact of being homosexual is usually a life problem, to be sure, but it is in no way a defect.

The other idea also devalues homosexuality, but in a moral sense. It could be expressed in a simplistic phrase: "Homosexuals are depraved." That means these individuals deliberately seek after evil; their will is morally perverse, which comes out in their choice of sexual activity which is against nature. Now this is radically false. The psychoaffective condition which involves having homosexual tendencies is never the result of choice. Moreover we have seen in chapter 2 that the reference to "nature" is dubious. It is clear that the homosexual situation involves moral problems; so do all human situations. But these problems are not of the kind implied by the term *depravity*. We will come back to this moral question for a more thorough analysis.

Homosexual people do not usually experience their situation as either a defect or depravity. They may have some trouble dealing with the facts, but they cannot wish them away. It is hardly surprising that some of them are rebelling against the widespread mentality I have been suggesting.

The trouble is that they may err in the other direction; trying to compensate for a deep sense of inferiority, they may overvalue homosexuality as a refinement or superior form of sexuality. It is not easy to find a way between this error and that of the widespread mentality: to consider the fact of homosexuality as quite simply a fact, one which is problematical, but hardly a question of value. "Not easy," however, does not mean "impossible." This book is an attempt in that direction.

One phrase has come up often during recent years: homosexuals want to be able to "come out of the closet." I feel this is an absolutely legitimate demand; between camouflage and exhibitionism there must be room for simple honesty. Let's strive, at least, to get there.

The Moral Question

It is asked all the time, but in various ways. Most often it comes in the form of uneasiness, even torment. Is it some mysterious punishment to be homosexual? A moral defect? A fault? In any case, whether alone or with partners, it leads to behavior which is charged with deep feelings of guilt.

Sometimes this guilt is expressed in roundabout ways. The person makes a strongly worded expression of nonguilt which generally sounds like a defense mechanism. We know what such vehement denial means. If a man declares in a certain tone, "That idea would never have occurred to me," he makes it quite clear that it has occurred to him, and that he is protecting himself.

The question of homosexuality cannot be morally indifferent. But we must examine very closely and methodically certain well-established beliefs inherited from the moral outlook of the past. I know I run the risk of offending two kinds of readers: those who hold this moral outlook so firmly that they consider it infallible and untouchable; and those who protect themselves from their own unconscious panic by vigorously denying that there are any moral issues at all. I want to contribute what I can toward freeing our thinking from both kinds of preconceptions.

First of all I must again stress that the fact of being homosexual is not a moral issue. It is neither a fault nor a sin nor a vice—it is a fact. No individual chooses to have homosexual tendencies, so it would be stupid and unjust to criticize anyone for having them. Sexual tendencies are a given which people have to get along with in one way or another.

Today we know that the primitive origins of this given are psychological more than biological. But in any case homosexuality develops totally outside any moral consciousness, simply because it develops before any clear awareness of the "I" who acts.

Is the fact of being homosexual *bad*? The term is highly ambiguous; it suggests both a judgment of moral value, and a judgment of well-being which is purely descriptive. That homosexuality is bad in the second sense is obvious. Of course some homosexuals don't experience their situation as a life problem, a malaise, a source of suffering, yet I wonder more and more if this attitude is not their only defense against overwhelming anxiety. I have also become more and more convinced that most people who live with homosexuality feel very differently. In terms of full sexual development, the problem of homosexuality really is bad, like a psychological birth defect (though not like a defect in the congenital sense that must limit human potential). People experience the problem in different ways; they may adjust to it rather well, or struggle with it unsuccessfully. But the fact of being homosexual is in no way *morally* bad.

At the same time there are issues to consider. The fact that a person is homosexual—which is not a moral question—is going to pose problems of behavior which do call for moral appraisal.

Jacques falls in love with Pierre, or Françoise with Jeanne. Can we call this a sin? It would clearly be absurd to say yes. Passion is not aroused voluntarily; it is suffered passively, as the word itself suggests. This burst of feeling, perhaps triggered by no more than a glance, has been described as far back as the Song of Songs in the case of heterosexual love. This too is a fact, an intense reality that imposes itself regardless of the will or choice of the people involved.

The feeling of passionate love is complex and virtually indescribable. There is a desire to be with and know the other, to create a lasting intimacy. There is a desire to live this intimacy through physical closeness and mutual erotic expression. I think it is very rare that a feeling of love dispels erotic desire, as in the case cited in chapter 1. Yet a desire that wells up suddenly and

irrationally cannot be considered a moral act, either good or bad.[2]
As for the *feeling*, how can the fact of loving someone be bad,
unless of course this someone is loved as an object to be possessed.

On the other hand, what about the man, in the unbearable
loneliness of his evenings, who feels driven to go out and find
a partner who is willing, temporary, and anonymous? This, too,
is hardly a moral act; the man suffers an urge which he can
not prevent, and may not, in the long run, be able to master.
People have often told me of these overwhelming drives, with
which they may struggle for hours, in vain.

Up to this point there can be no question of fault or of sin.
Passions and drives are not moral facts, but psychological facts.
Yet they tend toward some erotic expression. For convenience
let's retain this dichotomy of passions and drives, with the understanding that they can and often do coexist in the same individual. The question then arises of the moral value and implications
of human behavior.

It is here that I believe we must introduce a basic change in
outlook. The morality we call traditional leads to an insoluble
contradiction, a total dead end. To show how, I will use the
very language of this "morality." All genital activity belongs to
the domain of "grave matter"; that is, whatever is not "in order"
is "mortal sin" and "leads to hell."

All genital activity which is not directly aimed at procreation
is against this order, "against nature," and therefore "mortal sin."
The man must deposit his sperm *in vasum naturale*—we say it
in Latin, out of modesty—that is, in the vagina not just of a
woman, but of his own wife. This notion led to the condemna-
tion of artificial birth control; it was "against nature," an attempt
to "frustrate the marital act." From the standpoint of this
materialistic, legalistic morality, sexual problems do not exist so

2. We will come back to the problem of desire as suggested by the words
of Christ in Matthew 5.

long as intercourse takes place *in vasum naturale* between a man and a woman with the consent of the parish priest.[3]

It is thus clear that *all* homosexual genital activity is "mortal sin," since by definition the sperm is ejaculated anywhere *but* in a vagina. Yet there is a clinical fact that cannot be denied. The less a person's sexuality has managed to grow through normal relationships (see chapter 2)—this is true whether the tendencies are homosexual or heterosexual—the more difficult it is to control. Continence, though the individual may strongly wish for it, becomes all the more unreachable.

So people with homosexual tendencies are confined to total and permanent celibacy. Most of the time, however, they cannot achieve it, even if they try with all their will. Whether alone or with others they are drawn irresistibly into sexual arousal ending in orgasm. Since that cannot fail to be mortal sin, they are automatically destined for hell without having willed their sins. This sketch may sound like a caricature, but it is just where this kind of morality logically brings us. According to this logic, a man who is homosexual has only one solution: to kill himself right away to avoid hell. But suicide, too, is a mortal sin. For him there is no escape.

I don't think I have to carry this any further to show that this way of thinking must be rejected from the standpoint of simple humanity, and even more so from the standpoint of Christianity. Of course for practicing Catholics there is always the possibility of confession. But that leads to a sort of ritualistic repetition: they promise not to do it again and receive absolution, knowing all the while they won't succeed; then they start doing it again, compulsively, in spite of themselves. Running back and forth between the urinal and the confessional becomes absurd—in the long run it is the confessional that will cease to be frequented.

3. You can even read in some old handbooks of morality that the sex act is "a sin permitted in marriage for the purpose of having children."

For believing Christians this can be a real tragedy, for the very
basis of this notion of morality is false.

What is the standard used in making these moral value judgments? By what criteria can behavior be judged good or bad?
For traditional morality—whether denominational or not—the
criterion is "Nature" in some form or other. Certain kinds of
sexual behavior are "against nature": masturbation, anal and
oral intercourse, etc., anything that puts the sperm somewhere
other than in a vagina open to the possibility of fertilization. All
homosexual activity is by definition against nature.

Today, however, this notion of nature seems debatable. First
of all, it reduces everything to the one aspect of biology, and a
prescientific biology at that: as if sperm is a liquor of the gods
which contains the child. In spite of its spiritual facade, this
way of thinking is truly materialistic. Then too, this "Nature"
is somehow divinized in the eighteenth-century style of Rousseau.
It is a goddess whose will it is dangerous—even "mortal"—to
oppose. Many Christian theologians have fallen into this trap
while preserving their internal logic: they view "Nature" as the
manifestation of the will of God, without realizing that they have
reintroduced the age-old myth of the One Who Knows. The whole
Bible is oriented toward dispelling this gnostic myth.

Modern anthropology tends to rely on a very different criterion
of value. What seems positive and morally valuable is whatever
leads toward a fuller humanization, or at least does not stunt
human growth.

Now it is clear that in the human species the sex drive is only
minimally affected by the cycle of fertility. Among both men and
women, sexual desire is something more than physiological
rutting. If no female animal will mate while pregnant, it is
another matter among women. The human brain is radically
different from that of even the higher animals. It involves an
organizing sector, the orbital-frontal lobe, which performs no

physiological function. It has some other function, because human life goes beyond instinct and conditioning, beyond what we call nature. And so we have been called "denatured animals." Nature cannot be the ultimate criterion of moral value for judging human behavior. The question of value itself can only be posed by the human conscience, which is beyond nature.

In modern psychoanalysis, not psychoanalism, the criterion of value is again the goal of humanization. Here the standard really means the capacity for interpersonal relationship. Now let's consider the sort of relationship which is successful, and thus morally valuable: two people mutually find and develop within their relationship an understanding of themselves and of each other as individuals, not as things to be absorbed or rejected. It is a relationship through which they wind up being themselves, happy with their own identities—at least as much as before, and preferably more so. This is not an individualistic notion: each of these two people has many other relationships in life; for their own relationship to work, each must be fully sensitive to the other's complex role in the wider society.

In its deepest sense, and in the light of psychological thinking, this commandment to become fully human is still most clearly stated in the gospel: "You must love your neighbor as yourself"; "Always treat others as you would like them to treat you."

Here we suffer from a real poverty of language: we have only one word—love—for this basic commandment to value human life, and for certain emotions that may have nothing to do with it. Thus only in the psychological and evangelical sense of the "successful interpersonal relationship" can we clearly affirm that the true moral standard is not "nature" but *love*.

Pleasure can be an expression of love, when it is experienced within a successful interpersonal relationship. Sharing a good meal together is a pleasure; this pleasure is the place of friendship, that is, of love. Sexual pleasure can also be the place of love, in the true sense of the word. This is the real meaning of eroticism, which has nothing to do with the emptiness of pornography. Our culture is just starting to rediscover the importance of the erotic after a period of prudery and repression. Erotic pleasure does not necessarily express love: it may be solitary, and it may be sought with a partner who is viewed as an object, a means of arousal and release through orgasm; but it can be a sign of a true interpersonal relationship.

Homosexual men and women cannot be attracted by this pleasure except with someone of their own sex. That, as we have seen, shows an incomplete affective development, an imperfect access to the other. But they can't help it. Suppose a man in this situation has an erotic relationship with a partner who is also homosexual. At the level which is accessible to them, this could be a true interpersonal relationship. Now, is this a sin? Let's consider some examples from clinical experience.

Pierre, twenty-five, is in love with Paul, twenty-three, and vice versa. Neither of them feels any attraction to women. An affair develops; each partner may continue his usual lifestyle, or they may start living together as a household. It is then possible—in terms of the psychosexual state which is theirs without having willed it—that this liaison becomes a true interpersonal relationship, and that its erotic side expresses real love. It is also possible, just as with a heterosexual couple, that it is no more than a reciprocal utilization: each uses the other for his own pleasure or security, with little concern for that other as a human individual. The real moral criterion is at this level.[4]

Clinical experience leads me to believe that a successful homosexual pair involving real love is rare, especially on a long-term

4. We must not forget that homosexual practices are condemned in the Old Testament and by St. Paul because they were linked with idolatry, with the worship of various "false gods" and with the rituals of such religions. None of the four Gospels mentions the subject.

basis. Rare, but not impossible. Two people can, in fact, establish a true friendship which is their only possibility of opening up, of escaping the unbearable loneliness. Speaking as Christians we may well ask ourselves: where is the sin? Their situation is in no way comparable to a marriage, a term which implies sexual difference and the dimension of fertility. But it is a real situation in which people live as best they can, asking only that it not be condemned by those around them. In all honesty, this demand seems legitimate. For those involved, the relationship is the best they can envisage. How many times have I heard people who long just to be able to reach this point; they were weary, discouraged, bitterly disappointed in a moral sense from furtive or transient encounters in which the search for a true interpersonal relationship led nowhere.

Yet the problem of these furtive or transient encounters also needs rethinking. Here is the story one of my clients told me about his own personal evolution. He was about forty; I saw him three or four times a year for discussions that were spiritual rather than psychotherapeutic. Certain evenings he found himself driven to go out to a neighborhood known as a meeting place. He was full of guilt and inner turmoil, but the young gigolos were easily available and his drives were overpowering. He would go with some boy to a cooperative hotel in the area, quickly make use of him to have an orgasm, and take off as fast as possible, leaving him the price agreed upon. What really tortured him afterwards was that he had treated the boy—a human being like himself— literally as merchandise.

Then he began, with some effort, to try and establish real communication during these evening encounters. He wanted the boy, when they parted, to feel that someone had considered him for himself, not for the curve of his buttocks or the firmness of his muscles. From then on he began to discover the tragedies of childhood and adolescence which had led these boys in their late teens and early twenties to this way of life. Then many things changed. More and more often the conversation would continue even in the hotel room; the boy talked of himself, and the man, at first strongly aroused, felt a growing affection in which the eroticism faded.

Among many incidents he confided to me, I will always remember two. One evening, in a hotel room, he tried to tell his partner why his excitement had subsided and he no longer wanted to "enjoy himself." The boy spontaneously offered the explanation: "Ben, it's because you respect me." Another time the gigolo had stated his price and they had gone first to have a drink at an outdoor cafe. The boy seems to have been especially attractive. The conversation went on and on; the boy was delighted to be able to confide in someone who would listen to him. Then my client left him, giving him his price and wishing him "good luck." The boy was stunned; as they parted on the sidewalk he paused and exclaimed: "Well! This is a red-letter day. For once somebody gives me money without asking anything in return." Back at his own place, the older man went to bed and slept without even the desire to masturbate. He felt at peace, he told me, still thinking about the boy and wondering what would become of him. It seems obvious that this man had managed to transform his homosexual encounters—even if they sometimes had erotic elements—into something other than "sin."

Now if we turn to the meaning of heterosexual relationships, we find that the moral issue is analogous. The value of any act of sex is judged by the same criterion. Is there no sin at all in the attitude of the husband who forces intercourse on his wife when she doesn't want it that day; or who pays no attention to her fear of another pregnancy, and refuses to discuss the problem of contraception? Where is the love, in the gospel's sense, in such an attitude? And what of the heterosexual man who for social or economic reasons marries a not-too-disagreeable woman—and makes use of her for having children, but goes from mistress to mistress for his own pleasure? What concern does he have for his wife as a person?

It is shocking, in fact, to see that such a man enjoys a sort of reprobation tinged with indulgence (or even silent approbation) from those in the know. At the same time, two homosexuals who live together, striving for mutual help and fidelity, may be considered outcasts. This kind of hypocrisy is fading, at least in some circles. But there is a long way to go before we develop a truly moral approach.

Two more points should be made regarding the moral question from a specifically Christian (but not just Catholic) point of view. The first concerns the role of the confessor, the director of conscience, the spiritual counselor. Of course there is a difference between the Catholic confessor and the Protestant minister, but in this case it is rather superficial.[5] The homosexual man who comes to either of them is not asking for treatment to make him change; he is asking for help in his moral life and in his faith. If the counselor is dominated by a moralism based on the dubious ideal of nature he may do more harm than good. My clients have told me many stories of the sort. But if the counselor knows something about the problem, or simply knows and cares about human beings, he can help a great deal.

There can be a true "helping relationship" along the lines described above. In the Catholic context I have had the impression for ten or fifteen years that many more priests are using such an approach with their homosexual penitents. They are helping them focus their examination of conscience on the human quality of the relationship, not on false guilt over their tendencies. This is not psychotherapy, and I believe that priests and ministers should clearly understand this. Psychotherapy is not their job as

5. I do not have enough experience with what happens in the Jewish religion to speak of it accurately.

spiritual counselors, and it is not usually what their visitors want of them, but the help they do provide can be significant if they know their own role. If they are asked more specifically for psychological help, they can always refer people to a good psychotherapist while continuing to work with them in the context of their own helping relationship.

A second point concerns a passage from the Gospel of Matthew; it has sometimes been misread as an expression of neurotic guilt. Christ says: "You have learnt how it was said: You must not commit adultery. But I say this to you: if a man looks at a woman lustfully, he has already committed adultery with her in his heart" (Matt. 5:27–28).

This statement must be placed in its real context. From the biblical point of view, adultery is an act of injustice. It is not the sexual act that is condemned, but the fact that the one who commits adultery steals another man's wife; and the wife, who belongs to her husband (we are in a patriarchial Near Eastern society), consents to this theft. What is important in the gospel, however, is that Jesus puts true morality at the opposite extreme from Phariseeism and legalism: true morality is in the heart, not in the observation of laws, even just laws. It would be false to see his words as an anxious reinforcement of a superego which had been overshadowed by the rules of conduct. The passage is basically concerned with the internalization of the ethical life.

Thus it is not impossible that homosexual relations, though imperfect in terms of the full meaning of sexuality, may express an attitude in the hearts of real individuals which is positive.

The Homosexual and Faith

Love is always tragic—whether or not it is lived at the level of sexual expression.

This assertion may sound shocking and pessimistic. Yet it is merely a statement of fact, at least if we use the word *tragic* in its true sense. It is the human condition itself which is tragic: with each birth, a unique human history begins, obscure at first, then conscious—one story among the others. And the search for happiness is everything. But what is happiness? The pursuit of happiness? We pursue when we catch sight of something that corresponds in some way to our deepest desires, but which still escapes us. It is no chimera. The chimera is not happiness, but believing we have finally attained it, or that we can ever attain it fully, completely, in time. For this is a contradiction. Nothing can be complete while we are caught up in the passage of time— in change, frailty, and incompletion. Of course I don't mean we cannot be happy in life. The tragedy is that while time moves on, our happiness must be incomplete; yet only through time can we glimpse and pursue it at all. In the end, it is death which poses the real question of happiness, since that is where the passage of time leads.

Another common illusion is that somewhere there can be a human being who is perfectly complete, whole, totally at ease in all relationships. After all, if it were possible for such a person to exist, he or she would not be fully happy unless all the other human beings to be encountered in a lifetime were all, themselves, perfect. Obviously, then, no one would ever suffer. If only, that is, there were always sunshine or rain just when everybody wanted it; if it were never too hot or too cold, according to a universal consensus on the ideal temperature; if there were no mosquitoes, or snakes, or carnivores, or germs, or viruses; if there were also no fanatics who one fine day would invent some marvelous gadget to simplify your work, leaving you, in spite of yourself, its slave. If only . . .

This is the age-old chimera of the earthly paradise. The end of the twentieth century is scarred by the cruel disillusionment that afflicts humanity whenever it lets itself be charmed by this fantasy.

We are all neurotics. We know it, too—unless we can't deal with the sort of frank self-knowledge Freudian insights have made possible. Of course I don't mean neurotic in the pathological sense; relatively few people are neurotic to the extreme that calls for therapy. Human beings are, however, basically insecure about their happiness and their very survival. Among all living species, our own is characterized by this uncertainty, by this anxiety perpetually welling up, by this anguish over the course of destiny. The result is "religion" in all its forms, which Freud quite accurately called the obsessive neurosis of humanity. "Religion" is an inevitable, ritualistic, repetitive process. While it may be organized around a variety of myths, there is always some idea or other which corresponds to the Greek root *theos*, even, or especially, in so-called "a-theist" ideologies.[6] Humanity itself is sick. We must always place the homosexual question in this broader human context: It is the heartsickness of living in time and dreaming of a world without end which would no longer be just the passage of time.

In its truly Christian sense the word *faith* suggests something else. Faith is a dimension which is freed of the world of myth, or at least an attempt in that direction. In Christianity there is no longer just a hope; there is an expectation and a strange acceptance of time which does not last, which gives way to the end of time in death. Christ died in the throes of total defeat and radical despair, if we believe the texts. In that way he revealed himself as the Word of the other world—the realm of Love. Whoever believes in him prepares and waits for something else, which cannot be conceived without falling back into the prison of myth.

6. As Péguy said: "A metaphysical negation is an operation in the same category as a metaphysical affirmation."

Each person's life is a unique journey traveled in common. The way is full of conflict and suffering: even though suffering has many faces and shows them erratically—often with some people, rarely with others; even though it is instinctively rejected; even though it is almost always integrated in the long run. And when it isn't? Wouldn't suicide be an extreme, paradoxical, unconscious act of faith?

Here I'll pause to consider two crucial passages from St. Paul. But first of all, who was St. Paul?

The texts we have—his letters and the story of his travels—give us a glimpse of a man who really, intensely existed, a unique personality. But we cannot, in fact, know very much about him. Some writers have blundered onto the notion that we can psychoanalyze the dead; they have developed rather wild diagnoses that tell us more about their own problems than about Paul's. What we do know is that Paul was a deeply tormented man. He changed one day from a religious fanatic, a persecutor loyal to the Sanhedrin, to the faith of the Christ whose disciples he had been persecuting. What seems just as clear is that, while his attitude had totally changed, Paul's psychological makeup had not changed at all. He was still tormented and impassioned. It was no doubt his very suffering which brought him out of the religious prison of fanaticism and caused him to throw himself into announcing and spreading the message of Christ.

At least this is what comes to mind on reading the first passage: Romans 7:15–25. ". . . I cannot understand my own behavior. I fail to carry out the things I want to do, and I find myself doing the very things I hate . . . for though the will to do what is good is in me, the performance is not, with the result that instead of doing the good things I want to do, I carry out the sinful things I do not want. . . . What a wretched man I am! Who will rescue me from this body doomed to death? Thanks be to God through Jesus Christ our Lord!" I have quoted only the lines which relate

directly to my subject. This is a cry that all human beings, if
they are honest with themselves, utter at one point or another. The
human condition is divided in this mysterious impossibility of
performing the good that is willed. It would be entirely false, I
think, to limit the scope of these lines to the sexual aspect of the
search for the good. They tell of our fundamental human misery,
and of the hope which enters through the reference to Christ.[7]

But what was Paul's own problem, the source of his personal
suffering? It is a question that has been debated for nearly two
thousand years.

On this point we must turn to another passage where Paul
clearly mentions his secret, though he does not define it. In 2
Corinthians 12:1-9, he describes his inner enlightenment when
he is struck by Christ's words of love. Then: "In view of the
extraordinary nature of these revelations, to stop me from getting
too proud I was given a thorn in the flesh, an angel of Satan to
beat me and stop me from getting too proud! About this thing, I
have pleaded with the Lord three times for it to leave me, but
he has said, 'My grace is enough for you: my power is at its best
in weakness.' So I shall be very happy to make my weaknesses my
special boast so that the power of Christ may stay over me."
Remember that he wrote this some ten or fifteen years after the
death, in human ignominy, of the Christ to whom he refers. Paul
uses the figurative language of his times. He does not specify the
nature of this thorn in the flesh; he tells us only that it is his own,
and that it keeps him from forgetting, in the exaltation of a certain
saintliness, that he is of the same clay as everyone else: divided
and subject to weaknesses.

It is a question that has always troubled the commentators;

7. For a deeper analysis of this text and several others on human suffering, see part 3 of Sin (La Culpabilité), by M. Oraison (New York: Mac-
millan, 1962).

we have no scientific way to settle the debate once and for all. The "modern" interpretation, however, seems highly unconvincing: Paul's suffering is supposed to be an opthalmic ailment, or malaria. These syndromes were so common in his time that it is hard to see how Paul, in the context of this passage, could ascribe such importance to them. On the other hand we can catch glimpses of Paul's character through his writings—quite apart from what he says of Christ, his message, and his call. Paul had a sort of ardent affection for Barnabas, perhaps also for Mark. The way he speaks of these relationships cannot help but evoke the story of David and Jonathan, though in a very different historical context. Then again, Paul shows no sign of having been attracted to women, though we should not exaggerate the significance of this point. It is wrong to call him a misogynist (how do we know?), but we do not sense in him the rapport with women of a man for whom heterosexual love was possible. Again, this is just an impression. It would be presumptuous to affirm— or to deny—anything categorically, but to the Greek commentators of the earliest centuries, this famous thorn in the flesh could be the pain of homosexuality. I wonder why this interpretation was gradually covered up, then replaced by the pious hypothesis of malaria?

We cannot dismiss the possibility that the personal suffering of Paul, the place of his encounter with Christ, was directly linked to the question of homosexuality. The same hypothesis would not even occur to us in the case of John, or Peter, or Luke, or Matthew, or James.

Prepare and wait. This should be the attitude of a Christian throughout life.

Prepare: that means to participate with all our strength, wherever we are, in the real, diverse relationships that make up our lives. To prepare for the fullness of the world of love. Love in the universal sense of the term, not only in its sexual form.

Wait: that means to go to the end of time—not to believe we are already there, not to let ourselves be taken in by the illusion of the earthly paradise, not to stop on the way from weariness or disillusionment.

In short, to keep on living like a fetus preparing to be born. The Christian life includes sexuality as a central theme, but it cannot be reduced to psychogenital activity. Life is a rough voyage, sometimes terribly trying: creativity fails, power and money oppress, loved ones die, the living are hard to love. A voyage . . . of course the image is classic. It is a voyage toward the other world, that unimaginable but longed-for world into which death leads. If we strip it of any negative and macabre overtones, the Way of the Cross is the phrase which best captures this idea. The walk of Christ is deeply symbolic of all human journeying. It starts with the will to love, to make love reign across the trials and failures of time. And in the end love conquers through the supreme liberation of death. Freed from the contradictions of passing time, we can reach the completeness without limit beyond all desire.

Each person follows his or her own way of the cross. It is like the ways of all human beings, and yet radically unique—solitary, communal, and convergent.

Speaking as a Christian, the Way of the Cross is the meaningful struggle to burst into real life. It is the opposite of any pious masochism. I will use the phrase in this Christian sense, for it would be false modesty not to proclaim such a daring hope.

There are personal crosses which are not of a sexual nature: failures, obsessions, inhibitions, anxieties, insoluble conflicts, problematical relationships.

There are heterosexual crosses. The sexual life can be neurotic. Psychoanalysis shows clearly that even with a truly successful couple, there are dark periods and crises which may also be the basis of growth. Then again, though we may want love in itself to be "im-mortal," people are mortal.

There are homosexual crosses. The homosexual condition itself seems especially revealing of the basic, universal human tragedy. Because suffering, after all, is subjective, there would be no point in stating flatly that homosexuality is more painful than heterosexuality. My experience suggests that this is true, but I have met men and women who apparently suffered more in their heterosexual condition than certain others in their homosexual condition. Here too the simple formulas do not fit reality.

In fact, human sexuality itself is mysterious and tragic in the positive sense of the word *tragedy*, like the word *cross*.[8] Sexuality tends to express itself and blossom in what I have been calling the enjoyment of the other. It is the mutual glimpse of self in the pleasure of relating to a fellow creature who is physically different.

But it never quite gets there in the real world of time. Not in a way that is completely free of the specters of the prerelational unconscious. Not even in the most positively successful heterosexual couple.

We have seen that the condition of a person with homosexual tendencies is rooted in the strange incompleteness of all human sexuality. Homosexual life is not something apart. It is one version, among others, of the fundamental human tragedy. This tragedy is a question beyond any scientific or rational explanation, yet through faith it acquires meaning. Through Christ triumphant in death, all suffering is revelation, birth, a personal Way of the Cross. So it is that a homosexual can say with all of us: "In my own body I make up what is lacking from the sufferings of Christ."

8. In *The Human Mystery of Sexuality* (*Le Mystère Humaine de la Sexualité*) I have tried to reflect on this huge question more than I have space to do here (New York: Sheed and Ward, 1967).

It is startling to return to the opening of the biblical text. Sexual duality is central. It is the place of likeness to Divine Love; but it is also the place of conflict and incompleteness. Such is the deep meaning of the first three chapters of Genesis, if we take them as the full articulation of themes suggested in myth.

Now let's compare the data of modern anthropology. Human sexuality is seen as the place where life renews itself, the place of love. But it is also the place where death appears, thwarting the innate wish for something beyond time. The most flourishing heterosexual love runs headlong into it—the brevity of the unifying orgasm, which can open only momentarily the dimension of timelessness; the inexorable mortality of self and other. This love is prolonged, of course, through fertility, but children themselves are immersed in the same incompleteness. The death of young ones shakes us to the core.

In the last analysis, what we find in human hearts and in the experience of sexuality is failure—something is always missing, and desire is never satiated in the world of time.

I hope my final point may be a wide open window, bringing light and fresh air to a subject that has long been hidden away. Through the faith of Christ, heterosexual men and women know that life is an ambivalent experience, and that they must walk through time with a sense of fundamental insufficiency. Through faith, homosexual men and women know that they participate in this same journey with an even more radical awareness of human failure. Together, as brothers and sisters, we all follow the way of the cross.